Praise for *The Space Between*

Matt Braddock is the real deal — deeply rooted in Christian faith, deeply engaged in the world. His book provides solid theory with a wealth of practical suggestions for deepening personal and congregational engagement on behalf of faith-based activism.

Anthony B. Robinson
Author of *Transforming Congregational Culture*

Putting our faith in action in the world requires grounding in spiritual disciplines. Overcoming evil requires that we not be worn down or co-opted by the darkness around us. Rev. Braddock has written a book I will carry in my back pocket to fuel me for the journey ahead.

Rev. Jen Butler
CEO, Faith in Public Life

In these intensely challenging times for our nation and our world, it is all too easy as spiritual activists to become consumed by the anger, polarization, fear and pain that swirls around us. The urgency of the work of justice wears us down to the bone, and we lose the connection to the transformative power within and among us. *The Space Between* is a much-needed reminder of the need to re-center ourselves, over and over again, in courageous compassion. Braddock offers practices for expanding our moral imagination, building authentic community and responding to the pain of the world with an open heart and an open spirit.

Sandy Sorensen
Director, Washington Office, United Church of Christ, Justice and Witness Ministries

Braddock has written a book that is the embodiment of the message he brings -- an invitation to find faithful ways to engage injustice and encounter the transcendent. It is theologically grounded and practically directed. It should be read by those who struggle with the paradox and possibility of spiritual activism, as well as those who never thought about it. A great book for community study and reflection, it is a manual for the spiritual activism our times so urgently require.

Rev. Dr. Stephen L. Sterner,
Former Acting President of the Pacific School of Religion & Executive Minister of Local Church Ministries of the United Church of Christ

The healing and restoring of the world happens through the liberating and courageous Spirit of love. The Spirit moves us toward prophetic action, compelling us to mobilize, provoking us to work for justice rather than watching as silent bystanders, and confronting systems that wound our sisters and brothers and violate God's creation. Matt Braddock adds his voice to a growing chorus of faith leaders who invite us to participate in the Spirit's patient and persistent love in action. Braddock helps both seasoned and newly-called faith activists go to the places of deep division and traumatic wounds to help us connect to God and one another. *The Space Between* will help you construct a reflective search for the loving justice of a living God.

Grace Ji-Sun Kim
Associate Professor of Theology at Earlham School of Religion. She is the author of over a dozen books, most recently, *Embracing the Other* and *Mother Daughter Speak*.

Matthew Braddock, modern-day contemplative and activist pastor, disrupts the religious right's hold as the arbitrators of God's will and divine actions in the world. He offers a powerful path forward on how we can be effective spiritual activists with left-leaning values, progressive views, and righteous expectations for a just world outcome, thereby transforming our churches, communities, and institutions. Rev. Braddock makes our sacred religious texts come alive in new ways of social activism that transcend fear.

Rev. Dr. Carolyn Boyd-Clark,
Chair, Committee on Global Actions / Concerns, National Board Of Directors, Church Women United, New York, NY

This book lures us beyond the unnecessary divisions we often create between our activist lives and our spiritual lives. Even congregations can sometimes segment rather than connect our contemporary social, economic and spiritual challenges. The author guides us on the path of being "spiritual activists" by providing thoughtful thematic reflections, prompts for conversations, and practices for cultivating active contemplation and contemplative action. This is a helpful resource for our time.

Dr. Lawrence Peers,
Congregational consultant and seminary professor

In genuine conversation you risk the possibility and the threat of conversion. In *The Space Between* Matt Braddock invites us to the "rest between two notes that are somehow in discord"—a "neutral zone"—where I can pull back from addiction to my way—to see another's. Braddock grounds the ideal with real conflicts as he explores these discordant notes: "the overlapping space between contemplative action and active contemplation."

Kent Ira Groff
A spiritual companion, retreat leader, and writer/poet in Denver, CO, Founding Mentor of Oasis Ministries in PA
Author of several books including *Clergy Table Talk, Writing Tides* and *Honest to God Prayer: Spirituality as Awareness, Empowerment, Relinquishment and Paradox.*
Contact kentiragroff@comcast.net

The Space Between is both inspiring and motivating. The author's concept of spiritual activism illuminates many of the challenges we face. It is a superb resource both for individual reflection and for congregational study groups.

David Smock, Ph.D., M.Div.,
Retired as Vice President and Director of the Religion and Peacebuilding Program at the U.S. Institute of Peace

Like the ancient Israelite and Judean prophets of 8th and 5th century BCE that remind the community to hear and obey the words of the covenant, to boundary shifting and collapsing systematic and constructive theological voices of yesterday and today, Matthew Braddock combines his erudition and pastoral sensitivity to call for a fresh social and religious activism – spiritual activism. In this well-researched, socio-theologically reflexive book, Braddock advances conversation to active contemplation. The subject matter is original. It explores faith agendas and progressive social movements for both community and individuals. Scholars, pastors, and lay will learn something new. Braddock's innovative work is highly recommended.

John Ahn, Ph.D.,
Assistant Professor of Hebrew Bible,
Howard University School of Divinity

The Space Between is a book containing big ideas. The Reverend Dr. Matthew Braddock (Pastor Matt to me) has written a timely book about the timeless tension and complementarity between action and spirituality. In covering everything from power to pity, his book offers no easy formula for how to reconcile the pursuit of justice with a spirituality that transcends everyday life. Instead Braddock provides a framework for reflection, a framework enriched by personal experiences as well as by scripture and other religious sources, and most certainly a framework for conversation and group study.

Clarence N. Stone,
Research Professor of Political Science and Public Policy, George Washington University

THE SPACE BETWEEN

SPIRITUAL ACTIVISM IN AN AGE OF FEAR

MATTHEW BRADDOCK

Energion Publications
Gonzalez, Florida
2018

Copyright © 2018 Matthew Braddock

Unless otherwise noted, Scripture quotations are taken are taken from the New Revised Standard Version Bible, Copyright © 1989 by the Division of Christian Education of the National Council of the Churches of Christ in the U. S. A. Used by permission. All rights reserved.

Electronic Editions:
Adobe Digital Edition: 978-1-63199-523-1
Kindle: 978-1-63199-524-8
iBooks: 978-1-63199-525-5
Google Play: 978-1-63199-526-2

Print:
ISBN10: 1-63199-511-1
ISBN13: 978-1-63199-511-8
Library of Congress Control Number: 2018935546

Energion Publications
P. O. Box 841
Gonzalez, FL 32560
850-525-3916

energionpubs.com
pubs@energion.com

DEDICATION

To the Sheiks of the Shifting Sands,
still spiritual activists after all these years,

and

Chris, my wife and partner
on the journey in creating a better world

TABLE OF CONTENTS

	Series Preface	vii
	Introduction	ix
1	Activism and Non-Resistance	1
2	Covenant, Conflict, and the Common Good	11
3	Is Non-Violence the Only Way?	19
4	Diversity: The Key to Resilience	31
5	Dismantling Racism	39
6	Compassion Is an Act of Resistance	51
7	Double Justice	59
8	Courage in the Public Square	65
9	Economic Life	75
10	Pity, Compassion, and Power	85
11	Isolation, Prayer, and Community Wisdom	93
12	Open Faith Communities	103
13	Faith Is a Verb	111
14	The Death of False Hope	119
15	Love: The Connective Current of Life	127
16	Concluding Thoughts	137

Appendices

A	What is a Covenant?	139
B	A Sample Just Peace Covenant	141
C	A Sample Open, Affirming, & Welcoming Covenant	143
D	A Sample Racial Justice Covenant	145
E	A Non-Violent Communion	147

Bibliography ... 151

Series Preface

Clergy, having left Seminary, quickly discover that there is much about congregational ministry that they never learned in school. They have touched upon it in a practical ministry class or a preaching class, and an internship may have allowed a person to get their feet wet, but as important as this foundational education is, there is much that must be learned on the job. It is not until one spends actual time in congregational ministry that one's strengths and weaknesses are revealed. Continuing education is therefore a must. Having collegial relationships is also a must. Who else but other clergy truly understand the demands of this vocation? In addition to ongoing continuing education and collegial relationships, it is helpful to have access to books and articles authored by experienced clergy.

This series of books, the second to be sponsored by the Academy of Parish Clergy, is designed to provide clergy with resources written by practitioners – that is by people who have significant experience with ministry in local congregations. The authors of these books may have spent time teaching at seminaries or as denominational officials, but they also know what it means to serve congregations.

The Academy of Parish Clergy, the sponsor of this book series, was founded in the late 1960s. It emerged at a time when clergy began to see themselves as professionals – on par with physicians and attorneys. As such, they not only welcomed the status that comes with professional identity, but they also embraced the concept of professional standards and training. Not only were clergy to obtain graduate degrees, but they were engage in ongoing continuing education. Following the lead of other professions, the founders of the Academy of Parish Clergy saw this new organization as being the equivalent to the American Medical Association or the American

Bar Association. By becoming a member of this organization one would have access to a set of standards, a means of accountability outside denominational auspices, and have access to continuing education opportunities. These ideals remain in place to this day. The Academy stands as a beacon to clergy looking for support and accountability in an age when even the religious vocation is no longer held in high esteem.

In 2012, the Academy launched its first book series in partnership with Energion Publications. This series, entitled *Conversations in Ministry,* fits closely with an important part of the mission of the Academy – encouraging clergy to gather in groups to support one another and hold each other accountable in their local ministry settings. The books in this first series are brief (under 100 pages), making them useful for igniting conversation.

This second series, *Guides to Practical Ministry*, features longer books. Like the first series, these books are written by clergy for clergy. They can be used by groups, but because they are lengthier in scope, they can go into greater depth than the books found the first series. Books in this series will cover issues like writing sermons, interim ministry, self-care, clergy ethics, administrative tasks, the use of social media, worship leadership.

On behalf of the Academy of Parish Clergy, the series' editorial team, and the publisher, I pray the books in this series will be a blessing to all who read them and to all who receive the ministry of these readers.

Robert D. Cornwall, APC
General Editor

Introduction

I am the rest between two notes,
which are somehow always in discord
because death's note wants to climb over –
but in the dark interval, reconciled,
They stay here trembling.

And the song goes on, beautiful.

~ Rainer Maria Rilke, from Book of Hours
(translated by Robert Bly)

It is hard to imagine the American civil rights movement, or any social progress over the last century, without the involvement of religious groups like African-American churches, the American Jewish community, or Mainline Protestant and Catholic Christian activists. A recent report by the Brookings Institution reminds us of the role of economic justice among faith communities. It says,

> Throughout American history, religious voices have been raised, forcefully and often bravely, on behalf of social reform. The movement against slavery was animated by the witness of Americans who were inspired by their faith. In the late 19th Century, young men and women witnessing on behalf of the Gospel's call for service to the poor entered the nation's slums

and began work in Settlement Houses. Many of them sparked the rise of the Progressive movement.[1]

Some of us still remember the "Nuns on the Bus" who preached on behalf of the poor and the marginalized and played a central role in the 2012 presidential election, or Moral Mondays organized by Rev. William Barber to protest government voter suppression in North Carolina.

While religious progressives have participated in and led social change and human rights movements, popular understanding of religion in the public arena recalls the Moral Majority, the Christian Coalition, and Tea Party religious conservatives who have become integral to the Republican Party platform. Many in the religious right have become steadily angrier about what they see as a growing secularism that undermines the Christian roots of American heritage. They think secularism warped Christianity and that the culture-at-large yokes the name of Jesus to ideas, beliefs, and attitudes that would have appalled him. Secularism, in their mind, is an irrational and illogical form of liberal fundamentalism that wants to undermine and destroy Christianity.[2] One result of the persistent voice of the religious right is the perception that one Christian point of view alone plays a powerful role in the Conversations of issues that roil our society.

Religious social movements have not enjoyed the same valence with Democrats and progressives. When it comes to liberal religious voices in progressive policy initiatives there is ambivalence at best, and exclusion at worst. Ignoring or excluding diverse religious voices may lead to the peril of the very programs policy makers try

---

[1] E.J Dionne Jr., William A. Galston, Korin Davis, Ross Tilchin, "Faith in Equality: Economic Justice and the Future of Religious Progressives" (Washington D.C.: Brookings, 2014), 6-7.

[2] For example, see David Robertson, "Comment: New Secularism Is an Attempt to Undermine and Destroy Christianity," *Christianity Today* (May 19, 2014), http://www.christiantoday.com/article/comment.new.secularism.is.an.attempt.to.undermine.and.destroy.christianity/37537.htm.

to enact. Along with Gallup polling indicating a growing social liberalism in America,[3] a study by Public Religion Research says that religious progressives already make up 28 percent of the Democratic party — this in addition to 42 percent that are religious moderates. These trends will grow as the so-called Millennial Generation ages and begins to vote in greater numbers. When it comes to economic issues, religious progressives are more passionate than other liberals about eradicating income inequality.[4]

Why is there is a disconnection between social and religious progressivism? It is partly because many people treat faith and religion as a private matter. It is also because the religious left feels silenced by the aggressive, unapologetic way in which the religious right delineates "true" Christians from "false" or un-Christian. And partly, perhaps, it is because religious progressives sense the danger of seeming superior and self-congratulatory in their professions of faith. While often aligned towards the same vision and values, social and religious progressives are, to borrow Rilke's words, two notes which are somehow always in discord.

Both social and religious notes are essential if we want to further a progressive agenda that creates equity and compassion, restores the dignity of all people, and ensures the full participation of all Americans in common life, common wealth, and the common good. This book explores the intersections of those seemingly discordant movements. Each chapter is an interpretive vehicle to help us explore and apply texts. Our "texts" are not just from religious sources like the Bible. Texts include all sources of meaning-making like personal history, racial and cultural constructs, educational

---

3   Jeffery Jones, "On Social Ideology, the Left Catches Up to the Right" (Gallup, May 21, 2015), http://www.gallup.com/poll/183386/social-ideology-left-catches-right.aspx?utm_source=Politics&utm_medium=newsfeed&utm_campaign=tiles.

4   Jack Jenkins, "The Rise of the Religious Left: Religious Progressives Will Soon Outnumber Conservatives," *Think Progress* (July 19, 2013), http://thinkprogress.org/politics/2013/07/19/2324411/the-rise-of-the-religious-left-religious-progressives-will-soon-outnumber-conservatives.

status, class assumptions, economic opportunity (or lack thereof), political perspectives, and so on. We are all interpreters of personal and community texts. Each chapter represents a way of asking, "How do our texts speak to us? How do we make meaning from them?"

This book also asks, "What do we bring to the reading of our various texts?" When it comes to the spaces between religion and social activism, is there coherence which may be deemed acceptable by social progressives and the religious left? The hoped-for outcome is that we can together read our diverse texts and interpret them in ways that demonstrate compassionate justice.

This book also explores the intersections of another set of discordant notes: the overlapping space between contemplative action and active contemplation. Along the journey of community transformation, religious sources help us hold both active and passive expressions of life and faith in balance. Community transformation requires active, tireless action as we confront the realities of exploitation, dehumanization, and suffering. Such confrontations can be painful, because they require a level of honesty about humanity's death-dealing ways. Growing awareness takes courage as we relinquish our biases and reunite dualistic perceptions. We are transformed by a mutual loving encounter in two dimensions: active effort and passive receptivity; works of compassionate justice balanced by open accessibility; insistent love tempered by the capacity to be loved in return. I call this "spiritual activism."

Spiritual activism is a breath … a heartbeat … a rhythm. We exhale, go into the world, and do the works of compassionate justice. We also know that we will not get it right the first time around. So, we gather back together and breathe in. We listen. We receive. We refine our approach. When we realize we cannot stay in our comfort zone continually, we exhale and head back out into our communities. We feed and house the poor. We clothe the naked. We visit the prisoners. We help those who live on the margins of our communities. We act together. And then we draw together to dream and listen for the breath of the Transcendent. Only then do we engage the community again. We act and then we listen. We move and then we pause. We progress and then we become still. Transformation comes in breath, heartbeat, and rhythm. It is passive and active.

Each chapter of this book explores a theme of spiritual activism which has caused discord between faith and civic engagement. At the end of each chapter you will find three opportunities to explore the space between the "texts." First, there are conversation questions for personal reflection and group study. Second, there are ideas for contemplative action. Third, there are some thoughts for active contemplation.

The reflections in this book mention statistics and social trends that were up-to-date for publication. While referencing data may erode the enduring relevance of this book, citing contemporary facts about the issues is crucial. We face the same problem with Web citations. Information on Webpages at the time of writing is accurate, but we know that digital locations change. Even though the data might shift from year to year, I am confident that the subjects raised in this book will continue to be relevant to future spiritual activists who seek to engage America's social challenges through faith-filled action.

This book is about reclaiming the dynamic movements of faith in social action. We will explore some principles for spiritual activism that seek transformation in the doing, the waiting, and the rests between discordant notes.

ACTIVISM AND NON-RESISTANCE

> Thrust back the evil of violence and set virtue on her seat again. ~ Bhagavad Gita

You may be familiar with this scenario: A mainline suburban church in financial straits plans a worship makeover to reach out to younger members. The pastor removes the U.S. flag from the sanctuary. The words "LGBTQ" and "global warming" appear in sermons and "gender orientation" is featured on the church website. Pastoral prayers, now addressed to "our Father/Mother God," are meant to convey open-mindedness. All this inclusivity and diversity should entice young adult worshippers, right? If so, then why is it that this once strong and large congregation now may not survive? One critique of liberal Christian traditions is that they preach and teach a path to growth through works of justice. However, while many local congregations in these traditions engage in hands-on social justice issues and reform their worship to align with their mission commitments, they are not experiencing renewal. Perhaps the lack of transformation illustrates the failure of religious progressives to link works of contemplative action with active contemplation that is necessary for the integration of spiritual activism.

The first quality of integrated spiritual activism is *satyagraha*. *Satyagraha* is a word invented by Mahatma Gandhi and his followers. It is a synthesis of two words: the word *satya* means, "truth founded in love," and the word *agraha* mean, "firmness, insistence and force." *Satyagraha* means a force and a power born in truth and love. Gandhi used the word to describe non-violent resistance to bring about change. Gandhi sometimes called it "love force" or "soul force." A *satyagrahi* is one who fights for the truth through non-violence.[5] *Satyagraha* is close to the spirit of the Christian Gospel, though sadly not lived often enough. *Satyagraha* means clinging to truth, no matter what. Under no circumstances can a spiritual activist hide or keep truth from an opponent. The spiritual activist is obligated to be honest, open, and direct in dealings with opponents. No matter the cost, one must follow the truth, even as she or he endeavors to be truthful.

On one level, *satyagraha* is the means to eradicating injustice using soul force rather than through violence or physical force. A spiritual activist is not out to conquer but to convert; not to prevail, but to persuade. She endures with infinite patience and humility. She does not bulldoze others, but takes the way of self-suffering. Gandhi believed that the spiritual activist derives her power from God. Dependence on God will help the disciple of nonviolence to develop the courage and fearlessness needed both to stay the course and to wear down opponents in the social struggle with love.

For Gandhi, Jesus was a supreme non-violent resistor. Martin Luther King Jr. noticed the same thing. Through *satyagraha*, King found a new way to affirm the teachings of Jesus, which spoke well to his people in his time and to some of us beyond.

In our faith communities, what do we make of the ideas like the soul force of Gandhi and the political resistance of King? What do we do with love and nonviolence in a country where power-politics reign supreme in our institutions, including religious establishments? What do we do when many of our institutions, including religions, marginalize or silence the voice of dissent to protect the status quo? Of what relevance is *satyagraha* at a time when only certain, media-curated social crises tend to shock the moral sensibility of political, civic, business, educational and religious leaders?

---

5   T.V. Philip, "Christian Spirituality (1 Corinthians 1:18-25)," *Religion Online,* http://www.religion-online.org/showarticle.asp?title=1539.

The Space Between 3

Think about those who have been deeply wounded by life. Think of those who have suffered most terribly, those who flee their homes in the face of violence and brutality, or those who feel like outcasts because of the violence of betrayal, suspicion and hatred. Shame and duplicity are common experiences of many people affected by tragedy, violence, and fear. Victor Frankl, who chronicled his experiences as a Jewish prisoner in a concentration camp, observed three psychological reactions experienced by victims of violence:

> An overwhelming sense of trauma and inability to come to terms with the horror.
>
> A sense of apathy and despair that nothing can be done, and nothing will ever change.
>
> Lastly and often later, feelings of moral deformity, hatred, bitterness, disillusionment, blame and an inability to relate or trust in humanity again.[6]

Spiritual activists insist that this is not a transcendent purpose for humanity. Violence begets violence. As Rabbi Brad Hirschfield points out,

> The Bible never says we shouldn't want revenge: wanting it is normal! Instead, it acknowledges that there is a real cost, even when something happens by accident. Indulging our inclination towards revenge is not such a good thing, however. The Bible tells us to be aware that while the urge for vengeance can be legitimate, acting on that urge is not.[7]

Spiritual activism liberates us from cycles in which violence beget violence. We are given a chance to disestablish cycles of revenge and brutality by participating in the suffering of God for the world.

---

6   Victor Frankle, *Man's Search for Meaning* (New York: Pocket, 1959).
7   Hirschfield, Brad, *You Don't Have to Be Wrong for Me to Be Right: Finding Faith Without Fanaticism* (New York: Harmony, 2009), 65.

In 2012, a friend invited me to see the opera *Satyagraha* by Philip Glass at the MET in New York City. After an exhausting week of ministry, I almost did not go. Since the orchestration is a tonal, repetitive poem that is close to four hours long, I worried I would fall asleep. But, as often happens, when we are least expecting it, we can get drawn into something life-altering and unforgettable; something so special that we long to hold onto the experience, repeat it, and remember it long after it is over. Yes, the music repeated itself, but in the way a beating heart is repetitive; like breathing in and breathing out; like waves of the sea revealing treasures in the sand. The music and images entered the audience's blood stream. We inhaled it and grew with it like a prayer or meditation. *Satyagraha* was persuasively beautiful. I left the opera feeling hopeful. I left feeling transformed.

Occupy Wall Street activist Noah Fischer wrote about his experience at the same opera, but from the other side of the doors of the MET. After being evicted from Liberty Park, Occupy protesters looked for ways to promote their message in other public spaces. Fischer decided to gather with hundreds of protesters who assembled on the steps of Lincoln Center, blocked off from the plaza by police barricades and heavy NYPD presence. When a few who dared to cross the barricades were arrested, there were shouts of, "Shame, shame, shame!" from some of the protestors. Occupiers took off their shoes, a Gandhian symbol of dignity, standing barefoot on the cold pavement. As *Satyagraha* ended, the elegantly dressed audience exited into the plaza to see a barefoot protest at the bottom of the grand steps. Occupiers called out to opera-goers in unison to join the protest, but the sight of the NYPD barricades seemed to paralyze them. Philip Glass, who attended the performance that night, suddenly popped up in the Occupy Wall Street assembly to read a statement on the people's mic. As Occupiers sat down, and the lights from a video camera illuminated his face, Glass called out the last lines of the opera, a passage from the Bhagavad Gita:

> *Mic check!*
> *When righteousness withers away*
> *And evil rules the land*
> *We come into being*
> *Age after age*
> *And take visible shape*
> *And move*
> *A man among men*
> *For the protection of good*
> *Thrusting back evil*
> *And setting virtue*
> *On her seat again.*

Fischer writes,

> Chanting along with Glass, whose music had been the soundtrack to my childhood, I melted into the crowd, my body vibrating to the shared voice, deeply encouraged by this ancient text. When I looked up, the opera audience had joined us. The buffer zone was gone. We were one big crowd—the 100%! The physical NYPD barricades still stood among us, but they were no longer barriers, absorbed now into our big warm body. Until late into the night we held our general assembly. The police stood offstage, now relaxed. Two separate spaces had flowed into one, protesters had become people again, and the police could then be people too.[8]

For those who think that justice means injuring those who injure us, error can be corrected by error, or evil can be vanquished by evil, spiritual activism and non-resistance help us join in common aims. We thrust back evil, set virtue aright, and claim our ability to tear down the barricades that keep us from one another, as Jesus, Gandhi, Martin, and so many others began and continue to do.

---

8   Fischer, Noah. "Occupying Tension," *Inquiring Mind* (2012), http://www.inquiringmind.com/Articles/OccupyingTension.html.

FOR CONVERSATION

Spiritual activists can feel frightened by the magnitude of people, events, and systems that threaten our well-being. Non-violence does not mean that we remain indifferent to the problems. Non-violence also fosters a sense of compassion and caring. However, what happens when it all becomes too much? We may shut down due to compassion fatigue — making too much emotional connection. Constantly serving the needs of others can exhaust us. One antidote is to cultivate an open heart. We can develop open-heartedness by allowing ourselves to fully experience the emotions rocking around inside. We focus goodwill toward ourselves with the following phrases:

> *May I be safe*
> *May I be peaceful*
> *May I be kind to myself*
> *May I accept myself just as I am.*

We can also ask some questions:

> In what ways does my activism and contemplation foster fatigue or anger in my life?

> In what ways does my contemplation and activism promote self-care, goodwill, energy, and compassion in my life?

FOR ACTIVE CONTEMPLATION

Rabbi Brad Hirschfield suggests an exercise in which activists see themselves in line with the traditions of mentors and champions.[9] Find pictures of spiritual activists you admire. Fasten their photos on a wall — along with a mirror. As you look at those pictures, can you see yourself as a spiritual activist in the making,

---

9   Hirschfield, 248.

ready to be on the wall alongside those other images? If a mirror on the wall next to the photos is too public, get a small mirror, look into your own eyes, and ask yourself some simple questions before you get into bed at night or when you wake in the morning: "In what ways was I the person I most longed to be today? What helped me to get there? In what ways did I fall short? What do I need in my life to do better?" Instead of being a symbol for narcissism, the mirror becomes a sacred object. If we do this practice long enough and regularly enough, we will not only see ourselves in the mirror. We will see the image of God. We will begin making choices to benefit that person.

FOR CONTEMPLATIVE ACTION: GET TO KNOW YOUR CONFLICT STYLE

Spiritual activists will, no doubt, encounter conflict along the way. It is helpful to know how you handle conflict, and how members of your faith community deal with differences. Read each of the following statements and rate each response according to your most probable action or choice in each case. (1) will be your first choice, (2) will be your second choice, (3) will be your third choice, etc. Rank all five answers.

1. You are about to go into a public meeting in which a new policy will be offered where there is much disagreement. Your perspective to this policy is quite different than the rest of the community. Resistance to the majority will likely annoy many of the people there. You are most likely to:

_____ a.   Stand fast for your position.
_____ b.   Look for some middle ground.
_____ c.   Go along with the wishes of the majority.
_____ d.   Remain silent during the meeting.
_____ e.   Try to re-frame the issue so that all sides can be included in the solution.

2. I would say the following about differences:

_____ a.   Differences are to be expected and reflect the natural order: some have resources and others have none, some are correct, and some are wrong.
_____ b.   Differences should be considered with the common good in mind. At times parties are obliged to lay aside their own views in the interest of the majority.
_____ c.   Differences serve only to drive people apart and their personal implications cannot be ignored.
_____ d.   Differences reflect the basic attributes of people and are largely beyond influence.
_____ e.   Differences are a natural part of the human condition and are neither good nor bad.

3. I would say the following regarding the nature of conflict

_____ a.   Ultimately, right prevails. This is the central issue in conflict.
_____ b.   Everyone should have an opportunity to air feelings so long as they do not block progress.
_____ c.   Conflict requires self-sacrifice, the placing of the importance of continued relationships above one's own needs and desires.
_____ d.   Conflict is one of the evils in human affairs and should be accepted.
_____ e.   Conflict is a symptom of tension in relationships, and when accurately interpreted, may be used to strengthen relationships.

4. I would say the following regarding the handling of conflict:

_____ a.   Persuasion, power, and force are all acceptable tools for achieving resolution and most expect them to be used.

The Space Between 9

_____ b.   It is never possible for all people to be satisfied. Resolving conflict means persuasion combined with flexibility.

_____ c.   It is better to ignore differences than to risk open conflict. It is better to maintain the basis of relationship than to risk it.

_____ d.   Impersonal tolerance is the best way to handle conflict.

_____ e.   Conflict resolution requires confrontation and problem solving, often going beyond the apparent needs and opinions of the parties involved.

Based on your answers, how would you identify your dominant conflict resolution strategies? Each of the lettered answers for questions 1-4 point to a common conflict resolution style:

a. Control or Competition (using power to win your position)
b. Compromise (finding moderate, mutually acceptable solutions)
c. Accommodation (neglecting personal outcomes for the sake of the other)
d. Avoidance (sidestepping, postponing, or withdrawing from conflict)
e. Collaboration (seeking assertive and cooperative settlements)[10]

You may find that one of these approaches is your dominant style. Are you satisfied with how you handle conflict? Are there skills you would like to enhance? How does your conflict resolution approach compare with others in your faith community? In what ways do your conflict resolution strategies enhance or subvert others in your group?[11]

---

10   For more explanation of these descriptions, see Norma Cook Everist, *Church Conflict: From Contention to Collaboration* (Nashville: Abingdon, 2004).

11   Adapted from S. Rice, *Non-violent conflict management: Conflict resolution, dealing with anger, and negotiation and mediation* (Berkeley: University of California at Berkeley, California Social Work Education Center: 2002).

2

COVENANT, CONFLICT, AND THE COMMON GOOD

When I meet with parents who want their children to receive baptism, I frame the ritual in terms of covenant. God calls us. We respond. The congregation witnesses, affirms, and supports the vows that are made. As we prepare, I ask parents to tell me what they think the word "covenant" means. Answers range from confused shrugs to "a place where nuns live." Some will state that a covenant is like a legal contract. Most do not think about a set of mutual promises that call us to faithful accountability while being sustained by God's grace. The metaphor of covenant can also provide a framework and vocabulary for spiritual activists to understand what it means to be faithful to God through active contemplation and contemplative action.

The Protestant Reformed tradition reminds us that God's covenant with Israel expressed God's love and offered an invitation to serve and love God in faithfulness.[12] Hebrew Scripture scholar Walter Eichrodt claimed that covenant provided Israel's life with a goal and its history with a meaning. In covenant, God created an atmosphere of trust and security in which called people could find the strength to willingly surrender to the aims of God. When God summoned Israel into a covenant relationship, the notion of an arbitrary and capricious God changed. People would now know

---

12   "The Confession of 1967" in *The Constitution of the Presbyterian Church (USA) Part I: The Book of Confessions* (Louisville: Office of the General Assembly, 2003), 9.18.

exactly where they stood with the God of Israel. From that came the joyful courage to grapple with the problems of life.[13]

When it comes to spiritual activism, we also remember that covenant has a political dimension. Liberation Theology reminds us that God takes sides in the struggle for justice. As Gustavo Gutierrez says,

> The God of the Exodus is the God of history and of political liberation more than he is the God of nature ... Yahweh is the Liberator ... The covenant gives full meaning to the liberation from Egypt; one makes no sense without the other.[14]

Covenant is a response to grace. God chooses a people so that the people might choose God. Even when the people fail to follow their side of the covenant, they are never without the promise of reestablishment and renewal. God gives identity to the people. God defends and establishes them, and invites them to grow in their ability to hear and obey.[15] Some of us get tense when we hear the word "obedience." Maybe it is because we tend to associate obedience with perfection, punishment, following rules, and even words like "shame" and "belittling." While an element of compliance and threat certainly exists in Levitical law, covenant invites people to obey God's prophetic call to compassionate justice, even imperfectly, as a way to claim that we belong to God and want God's love to be known in the ways we relate to one another.

Covenant can also bring unity. The covenant spoken by the God of Israel to Moses had formative power in that it unified disparate and loosely associated tribes around faithfulness to the will of God. Admission to the covenant was not based on kinship

---

13 Walter Eichrodt, *Theology of the Old Testament, vol. 1* (Philadelphia: Westminster, 1961), 38.
14 Quoted by Charles H. Bayer, *A Guide to Liberation Theology for Middle Class Congregations* (Eugene, OR: Wipf & Stock, 1986), 93.
15 John Bright, *The Kingdom of God* (New York: Abingdon, 1953), 28-29. Obey literally means "to hear." The English words "obey" and "obedience" come from two Latin words that mean "to hear thoroughly."

but the readiness to submit and vow oneself to the God of Israel.[16] Covenant secures a state of *shalom*. Through faithfulness to God, people experience a state of intactness that brings vitality in matters affecting the life of God's people.

The metaphor of covenant points beyond itself to the liberation and re-creation of new people. Covenant expresses the best we can be. God calls us into covenant community. God personally interacts with us as a community. God's aims for the community are expressed in norms like righteousness, devotion, and love. A community that learns the art of covenanting makes room for the diversity of God's many gifts and graces. Spiritual activists begin the work of reconciliation through talking, cajoling, praying, forgiving, crying, and laughing together in covenant community.[17]

Living in covenant community does not preclude conflict. Healthy conflict, defined as exploring our differences responsibly, brings creativity, energy and new alternatives to faith communities where once there might have been one triumphalistic rule of faith and practice. Healthy conflict offers an opportunity for growth only if the differences of the participants are valued and if people learn to practice civil and patient boundaries with one another.[18] Being human means that we will face times when we are angry, confused, or blind. Faithfulness to God can lead us into a narrative of gratitude — an ability to focus on the good things God does in our midst and not just on the ways we pull away from one another. As the Apostle Paul writes,

> Finally, beloved, whatever is true, whatever is honorable, whatever is just, whatever is pure, whatever is pleasing, whatever is commendable, if there is any excellence, if there is anything worthy of praise, think about these things.[19]

---

16 Eichrodt, 39.
17 See Mark Lau Branson, "Forming God's People," http://www.alban.org/conversation.aspx?id=2456.
18 Gil Rendle, *Behavioral Covenants in Congregations* (Herndon, VA: The Alban Institute, 1999), 47-48.
19 Philippians 4:8.

We tell plenty of stories that blame others for our problems. Paul calls us to another conversation. Narratives of covenant and community can lift us out of our ruts by allowing us to participate with God and one another in bearing our living traditions into the future.

The New Testament expresses the Church's understanding of covenant. Through Jesus Christ, God covenants with the Church. Christians acclaim God does not reject an old covenant in favor of a new one, but engrafts the Church onto the olive tree of Israel so that all may also be part of the covenant people of faith.[20] God's initiative calls us into community. God's expresses divine aims for the community in norms like righteousness, devotion, and love.[21]

But here is the thing about covenants; the promises are often so intense that it can feel impossible to consistently live up to them. We will fall short of our promises. What happens when we break covenant? Breaking a covenant is different than violating a contract. In a contract, if one party breaks the agreement it can be voided. Sometimes the offending party is penalized, but both sides may be released from obligations. Think of the early termination clause on your mobile phone contract. You can get out of it. You are going to pay big bucks, but once you shell out some money, the contract terms are over. A covenant is different. Covenants go on even when we fail to meet the terms. With each failure, the parties may renter the agreement with hope. Covenants are re-established with the intent of living up to them again.

My faith tradition, the United Church of Christ, can be described as a covenantal polity. While we are non-creedal and non-catechetical, we do establish boundaries around our common practice of faith by creating local covenants. When someone joins our church, there is not a standard set of beliefs one must profess. There is not a statement of faith one must obey. To be part of our church means to agree to a covenant. We do not care so much about

---

20 See Romans 11:17-21.
21 William L. Holladay, *Long Ago God Spoke: How Christians May Hear the Old Testament Today* (Minneapolis: Augsburg, 1995), 37-38.

what one believes, but rather how we relate to one another with norms like righteousness, devotion, and love. The most important question is not, "Do you believe what we believe?" but rather, "How do we treat our neighbor, that is, how do we show God's love to others?" We make enduring, deeply held promises about how we want to treat each other and work together. Our covenants come from the hearts, hands, and minds of our people.

The congregation I serve has a covenant as part of its constitution. It explains how we agree to walk in the ways of God's abiding love. Every Sunday morning, we open worship by reminding each other of our covenant. I say, "Here, we honor and celebrate people of all races, cultures, ages, abilities, sexual orientations, and gender identities." These words give shape to our identity and guide our behavior. It is one of my favorite parts of our worship service. One day, a member of our church who is gay pulled me aside and said, "I cannot express how much it means to me to hear those words every Sunday. I am constantly reminded that God loves me, and I belong." The faithful expression of our covenant becomes a form of reconciliation, inviting people into right relationship with God and one another.

My congregation also has three covenants that direct our spiritual activism. Our "Just Peace Covenant" reminds us of the mutual promises we have made to work for peace by seeking justice for all peoples. Our "Open and Affirming Covenant" speaks to our promise to welcome and affirm gay, lesbian, bisexual, and transgender persons to participate fully in the life of our congregation. Our "Anti-Racism Covenant" acknowledges our ongoing journey to develop and implement strategies to dismantle racism through our adult and children's education, our worship services, our mission giving, our business practices, and our community social action. Each of these covenants can be found in the appendices.

Just like any covenant, our social action covenants represent our ideals. The reality is we do not always do a great job at living out our mutual promises. Sometimes we allow ourselves to get offended by someone's behavior and we stop looking for the image of the Divine in the one with whom we disagree. Sometimes we fail to support peace. Sometimes we forget that a covenant is not a policy statement, but a promise about loving relationships. Sometimes we are afraid to face our biases and privileges, so we do not meet the challenges of our anti-racism covenant. But failure does not mean we give up. God is not done with us. We reevaluate. We ask forgiveness, when necessary. We reconcile with each other.

Covenant reorients spiritual activists in the direction of love. When we falter, we ask God to give us a new heart. We recommit ourselves to sharing a common human journey and we covenant to value what is similar among us over what separates us. We recommit ourselves to appreciating our unique dignity and gifts and we covenant to recognize and celebrate the variety of gifts among us. We recommit ourselves to creating a better world and we covenant to support and encourage our individual and common efforts towards its fulfillment. We recommit ourselves to remember that our lives are worthy of love and we covenant to help each other engage our communities' compassion. We covenant to value our human journey, to achieve a better world, to praise the mystery, and to engage in the practices of a faith.

For Conversation

Covenant building begins with defining community norms. Think of a time when your faith community combined individual talents in ways that enhanced your mission. What talents did others bring to the table? What did you achieve, as a faith community, that would not have happened if people were working as individuals?

Covenants have power when all who are affected and all who have insight lend their voices in forming a faith community's common identity. Imagine you hold the power to make inclusive decision-making the norm within your faith community. What would you need to do more of? What would you need to change? What first steps would you take to move your faith community in that direction?

For Active Contemplation

What words are used to begin your worship experience in your faith community? Is it more than, "Good morning"? Are there any expressions of your community values – anything that reorients you in the direction of love? Craft some brief statements that express the norms of your community's faith and action. Consider using them in your own personal devotional practices, perhaps as a breath prayer or mantra.

For Contemplative Action

If your faith community does not have a social action covenant, consider going through the process of formulating your mutual commitments in writing. A simple process of covenant construction is in Appendix A. Sample covenants from the congregation at which I serve can be found in Appendices B, C, and D.

3

IS NON-VIOLENCE THE ONLY WAY?

One of the longest-running distortions in Christian theology has been the attribution of violence and violent intent to the will and activity of God. But if God is truly revealed in Jesus Christ, and if Jesus rejected violence, as is almost universally believed, then the God revealed in Jesus Christ should be pictured in nonviolent images. If God is truly revealed in the nonviolent Christ, then God should not be described as a God who sanctions and employs violence. ~ J. Denny Weaver[22]

THE *HABITUS*: BE AGGRESSIVE!

Pierre Bourdieu (1930–2002) a French sociologist, developed a theory of how people in a culture develop conventions for how its members act in a given situation. He called this shared practical sense the *habitus*. The *habitus* represents deeply ingrained customs, skills, and behaviors that we possess due to our life experiences. The *habitus* is a complex mix of tastes, preferences, and learned patterns that help us decide instinctively what to do and how to respond. Think of the earliest form of the word habit. Meaning "condition" or "appearance," a habit was a garment worn by members of religious orders that covered their features and set them apart. In the same way, a culture wears an ethos, or *habitus*, that distinguishes its dominant way of being while obscuring alternate ways of acting in the world. The *habitus* makes social life

---

[22] J. Denny Weaver, *The Nonviolent God* (Grand Rapids: Eerdmans, 2013), 5.

possible. We know what sort of behavior is expected in various social roles and settings. Because the *habitus* exists below the level of consciousness, an entire society can be in the grip of a dominant way of thinking and behaving without ever being aware of why it is we do things the way we do.[23]

The *habitus* of the West is aggression. In times of crisis, it seems that we turn to hostility as the only alternative for conflict resolution. Consider some of the language we use around problem solving. We attack the problem, tackle the issue, take a stab at it, wrestle it to the ground, and get on top of it. If colleagues argue with us, we complain that they shot down our idea, took pot shots, used us for target practice, or killed us. Facing opposition, we back down, retreat, or regroup. Because aggression is the *habitus* of our time, we can easily experience it as a positive attribute. Parents and cheerleaders scream from the sidelines of school sports events, "Be aggressive!" Supervisors reward managers for aggressive timelines and plans. Dictionaries define "aggressive" as hostile action, but also positively as assertive, bold, and enterprising. These combative descriptions of relationships and problem-solving point to a startling conclusion: We experience challenges as war zones, we view competing ideas as enemies, and we use problems as weapons to blame and defeat opposition forces.[24]

According to the American Psychological Association, violence is an extreme form of aggression.[25] Some of European culture's most influential thinkers considered violence and aggression unavoidable and natural. Darwin saw aggression as an advantage for survival. The philosophy of Hobbes and the psychoanalysis of Freud asserted that aggression and violence are hard-wired into our political systems as well as the human psyche. Modern theologians

---

23 Grace M. Jantzen, "Roots of Violence, Seeds of Peace," *The Conrad Grebel Review*, 20:2 (Spring, 2002), 5.
24 Margaret J. Wheatley, Geoff Crinean, "Solving, not Attacking, Complex Problems: A Five-State Approach Based on an Ancient Practice" (2004), http://www.margaretwheatley.com/articles/solvingnotattacking.html.
25 "Violence," The American Psychological Association, http://www.apa.org/topics/violence/.

like Karl Barth believed in a corrupt human nature with, "a very deep-seated and almost original evil readiness and lust to kill."[26]

Is it true? Is humanity defined by aggression and doomed to live in spiraling cycles of revenge, and swelling violence? Or, does aggression saturate the Western *habitus* so much that our esteemed thinkers were unaware of how they projected an unexamined bias into their writings? If aggression is hardwired into us as a universal human experience, can we ever hope for lasting peace through non-violent strategies, or are they doomed to fail?

Fighting with Love

This leads to the inquiry of whether spiritual activists who promote unqualified non-violent resistance actually mean it. Some progressives say they are pacifists, but when pressed they will admit to believing in some version of just-war theory, accepting violence as a necessary evil. Consider the response to the attacks of September 11 by a Washington D.C. pastor who wrote in the *Washington Post*, "Until Sept. 11 I would have described myself as a pacifist. I grew up inspired by the nonviolent teachings of Mahatma Gandhi and Martin Luther King Jr., and my preaching consistently opposed the use of violence." He concluded that in an imperfect world, "resisting evil through violence may sometimes be a necessary evil."[27] Many people of faith arrive at a middle road, like that advocated by President Obama in this Nobel Award acceptance speech:

> We must begin by acknowledging the hard truth: We will not eradicate violent conflict in our lifetimes. There will be times when nations – acting individually or in concert – will find the use of force not only necessary but morally justified.[28]

---

26 Karl Barth, *Church Dogmatics*, Vol. III: 4 (Edinburgh: T&T Clark, 1958), 413.
27 Quoted by Ivan J. Kauffman, "Nonviolence Works — If Somebody Does the Work," *The Conrad Grebel Review,* 20:2 (Spring, 2002), 40.
28 Quoted by Richard Beck, "The Paradoxes of Progressive Political Theology: The Paradox Revisited," *Experimental Theology* (May 11, 2017),

Within this framework, our *habitus* supports peace through aggression. The use of professional soldiers for peacekeeping operations by the United Nations points to the contradictory nature of promoting peace through the employment of so-called peace enforcement.

> Peace enforcement involves the application, with the authorization of the Security Council, of a range of coercive measures, including the use of military force. Such actions are authorized to restore international peace and security in situations where the Security Council has determined the existence of a threat to the peace, breach of the peace or act of aggression.[29]

Perhaps fighting lovingly, or seeking justice with love, is the best our *habitus* can support. This may sound ridiculous at first. How can fighting with love be possible? On the precipice of World War II, Gandhi wrote a letter to Martin Buber, the Hasidic mystic and Austrian-born philosopher. Gandhi recommended that German Jews must protest Nazi authoritarianism with non-violence and civil resistance. Buber responded with a long letter, which explained how Gandhi did not understand the brutishness of the Nazis. For Buber, the Nazis would interpret passive civil resistance as further proof that Jews were indeed inferior and thereby validate the regime's continued violence. The question for Buber was not whether to fight, but how to fight. As Buber closed his letter to Gandhi, "There is nothing better for a man than to deal justly - unless it be to love. We should be able even to fight for justice - but to fight lovingly."[30]

---

http://experimentaltheology.blogspot.co.uk/2017/05/the-paradoxes-of-progressive-political_11.html.

29 "United Nations Peacekeeping Operations Principles and Guidelines" (New York: United Nations Department of Peacekeeping Operations and Department of Field Support, 2008), 18.

30 Martin Buber, "Gandhi, the Jews & Zionism: Martin Buber's Open Letter to Gandhi Regarding Palestine," *Jewish Virtual Library* (February 24, 1939), http://www.jewishvirtuallibrary.org/letter-from-martin-buber-to-gandhi.

Are there times when we must choose limited violence as a response to aggression? Can coercion ever be the best strategy to bring peace? Working for peace is flawed. No action we pursue is perfect in its motivation, and so no action we take will bring the perfect peace of God's fully-established Reign that we read about in the New Testament. That does not mean we have to wait until we are perfect to examine and question the *habitus* of aggression and act in ways that counter the dominant way of relating to the world.

Mennonite theologian A. James Reimer presented a middle way between the "Christian realism" of Neo-orthodoxy (as illustrated by President Obama's speech) and the Anabaptist peace ethic, which claims that love, not sin, is the human norm. Reimer's middle way involves "just policing," which aims to restrain evil and maintain order for the common good. Just policing provides an accommodation to the *habitus* of aggression. While just policing cannot avoid the use of violence, it can be guided by the responsibility to restrain those who seek to hurt the innocent. Just policing balances restraint with enforcement of the law, reminding citizens that they are responsible for their actions. Enforcement emulates an image of a just and caring God who "forgives us our sins, even our violence, without excusing them," since "the loving God is amid death and violence in ways that are not clear to us."[31]

Considering the evidence of unchecked, systemic police violence against Black lives in the United States, Reimer may be overly-optimistic concerning policing. He neglects to mention the abuses of policing, including whether police mainly protect privileged elites and their property, the realities of racial profiling, police brutality, and the level of violence promoted in the training protocols of officers.[32] However, we can give some credit to the idea that restraining evil sometimes calls for the use of force if it can be dispensed with restraint by non-military police. When we

---

31 Susanne Guenther Loewen, "Is God a Pacifist? The A. James Reimer and J. Denny Weaver Debate in Contemporary Mennonite Peace Theology," *The Conrad Grebel Review*, 33:3 (Fall, 2015), 329-330.
32 Guenther Loewen, 331.

use force to confront aggression, we must do so with a refusal to allow the oppressor to dehumanize the resistor, coupled with the refusal of the resistor to dehumanize the oppressor. We will address this more when we consider the concept of Double Justice in a following chapter.

While some people of faith say violent restraint is a moral imperative, I think *Satyagraha*, discussed in chapter 2, provides a persistent reminder that we do not have to give into the dominant ethos of conflict that frames relationships through the language of dominance and aggression. *Satyagraha*, the growing of soul force instead of violent force, is the best way I have found to articulate my understanding of the non-violent aims of God for the world as understood through the life, ministry, and teachings of Jesus. Peace through non-violence is the goal and the expectation. J. Denny Weaver, the Mennonite theologian quoted at the beginning of this chapter insists that God should not be described as One who sanctions and employs violence. For Christians, the cross critiques the *habitus* of aggression. The cross is a mirror that allows our cultures of violence to view the dehumanizing and illegitimate evil structures that crave dominance of the human soul, not to mention the human addiction to violence. Looking at the cross, we have choices to make. We can turn away and allow the violence to continue through our silent complicity. We can participate, intentionally or unintentionally, in the unjust structures that kill innocent people. Or, we can choose to dismantle sin by repenting of our involvement and growing in the ways we incarnate God's love and peace. In their book on conflict in the workplace, Kenneth Cloke and Joan Goldsmith say conflict, "can be a source of inspiration, enlightenment, learning, transformation, and growth–or rage, fear, shame, entrapment, and resistance. The choice is not up to our opponents, but to us, and our willingness to face and work through them."[33] The same can be said of the cross. From the cross, God calls us to renounce victimization caused by aggression and to embrace

---

33   Kenneth Cloke, Joan Goldsmith, *Resolving Conflicts at Work: Eight Strategies for Everyone on the Job* (San Francisco: Jossey-Bass, 2005), xxxiv.

non-violence. How we choose to respond is up to us. From the cross, God calls us to embrace non-violence. That is the absolute truth as I understand it.

However, there is a conventional truth as well. While violence is ultimately an untenable response to conflict, we restrain those who pose a threat or cause danger. We do not want to be oppressed by the violence of others. Yet the price of counter-violence may be too high a price to pay for the feeling of safety. A radically nonviolent position is hard to maintain. Realistically, non-violent resistance does not work for every situation. If we choose to avoid or ignore those who commit violence, it only gets worse.

I do not think the conventional truth as we interpret it in the current *habitus* follows God's will, as we understand it through the cross. If we choose aggression to bring peace, we cannot justify it by either blaming or giving credit to God. It is arrogant and sinister when people use their religions to justify violence.[34] We have no choice but to take personal responsibility for our choices while also offering a critical evaluation and re-formation of our *habitus*. Violent language, control tactics, unjust social structures, and the biases which undergird the ethos of aggression must be acknowledged for what they are – detours from fulfilling God's aims for the world.

CREATIVE DESTRUCTION AND THE HABITUS OF MERCY

"Mercy" is the one expletives I hear from polite Southern women – one of those all-purpose exclamations for times when someone is too exasperated to say anything else. "Mercy me!" It works when you don't have the right words to say. Or, it is what criminals do in sentencing on T.V. police dramas: throwing themselves on the mercy of the court.

---

34   David Pratt, "War or Peace? Thinking Outside the Box," *Tricycle Magazine* (Spring, 2002), https://tricycle.org/magazine/war-or-peace-thinking-outside-the-box/

The Jewish scholars who translated the Hebrew Scriptures into Greek all those centuries ago had a hard time finding the right word for what we call mercy. For Hebrew and Arabic speakers, the idea of mercy is represented by the root *raham*. *Raham* is a womb-like state of love. Think about it as tender affection. Mercy is kindness or good will toward the afflicted, joined with a desire to relieve them. It has to do with sacred nurture and loving care. Mercy is not a feeling. It is not the same as pity. Mercy is a a give-and-get, pay it forward relationship.

Ancient Greek speakers used the word *elios* to represent the idea of mercy. It comes from a root word meaning oil that is poured out. When the Church sings the words *Kyrie Eleison,* we translate the phrase as, "Lord, have mercy." It is a prayer asking for the nurturing love of God to pour out upon us, like holy oil. The Biblical concept of mercy is to pour the same kindness on "the other" that God pours on us in our own "otherness." Mercy means having a pain in your heart for the pains of others, and taking pains to do something about their pain.

In the *habitus* of aggression, mercy is understood as weakness. Some perceive mercy as giving into feelings instead of following through with punishing offenders. But, for spiritual activists, showing mercy can become a way to disengage from the current ethos with a new way of being. We have all done things we regret. Aggressive things. Violent things. We have all had times when we wish we could go back in time and do something over again. The truth is, we all want mercy. But mercy is not given just so we can feel better. Mercy is not pity. God offers mercy as a way for us to restore our relationships. God offers mercy so that we can extend mercy to others.

In this present *habitus*, we must find the means to work and live together with non-aggressive strategies if we are to resolve the serious problems that afflict us. Mercy, far from being weak, has the power to destroy the ethos of aggression so that a new *habitus* may form. Margaret Wheatley, blogging on ancient Tibetan teachings, reminds us that destruction is necessary to life. Everything has its season. All things eventually lose their effectiveness and die. However, destroying comes at the end of life's cycle, not as a first response. As we become more aware of how the *habitus* of aggression affects our actions, we realize the cycles that have reached the end of their usefulness: outmoded beliefs; inappropriate or harmful values; traditional practices that no longer make sense; behaviors that support violence; programs that have outlived their usefulness; and policies that don't work as intended. As we dismantle our outdated, violent ways, we can establish a *habitus* of mercy.

Do you remember what Jesus said about mercy? "Blessed are the merciful, for they will be shown mercy" (Matthew 5:7). Jesus did not say, "Blessed are those who are shown mercy, for they will be merciful." In other words, Jesus does not say you get mercy and then you give it. Mercy is the primary intentional act. You are blessed for being a person who commits compassion. You get mercy once you give mercy. Spiritual activists can establish a *habitus* of mercy by pouring the healing oil of kindness and nurturing others in the womb of love. We must lessen our aggressiveness and increase our compassion, just as our God so often does with us. We give mercy. Then we receive mercy.

In my college days, I worked as a teaching assistant for an English professor at a small Evangelical school. One afternoon, Dr. Paul handed me a stack of papers to grade. As I read through the pile of freshmen English journals, I was disgusted by how poor the work was. Each passing paper was worse than the one before it, and the marks I gave reflected my loathing for their pasty writing. I delivered the graded papers back to Dr. Paul, shaking my head in disdain. The next day I went to his office. He had a stack of papers for me to look through. They were the journals I had corrected the day before. Dr. Paul had gone through and changed all the grades to higher marks. When I asked him about it, he simply quoted an OT prophet: "Matt, in wrath, remember mercy" (Habakkuk 3:2). That lesson has stayed with me. There is no doubt in my mind why Dr. Paul had a very devoted band of students on campus. Dr. Paul's authority was rooted in mercy.

The same should be true with people of faith. If we want to claim the authority to confront unjust systems and oppressive ideologies, then our *habitus* must be to be established by mercy. It is time for faith communities to destroy ends-justifies-the-means approaches to conflict. We have a role in deconstructing the *habitus* of aggression, and we do it through giving mercy before receiving mercy.

For Conversation

- How do you experience the *habitus*? Do you experience aggression and violence, or do you experience other forces? How would you name them?
- What is your first thought when you hear the word "mercy"? What does it evoke in you?
- Share a story about a time when you were able to give mercy before receiving mercy. As you tell your story, help the listeners understand what that experience was like for you.

For Active Contemplation

Recognizing our need to establish a culture of mercy only intensifies as we grow closer to understanding the aims of the Divine. Mercy awakens our appetite for compassion. In your prayer and contemplation, consider these cries for mercy from the Psalms. When you read them, imagine them as the cries of the oppressed asking for people of faith to establish mercy instead of aggression. How might this shift in perspective alter your understanding of the psalmists' words?

> *Answer me when I call, O God of my right!*
> *You gave me room when I was in distress.*
> *Be gracious to me, and hear my prayer.*
> – Psalm 4:1

> *Be gracious to me, O Lord, for I am languishing;*
> *O Lord, heal me, for my bones are shaking with terror.*

– Psalm 6:2

Be gracious to me, O Lord.
See what I suffer from those who hate me;
you are the one who lifts me up from the gates of death
– Psalm 9:13

Hear the voice of my supplication,
as I cry to you for help,
as I lift up my hands
toward your most holy sanctuary.
– Psalm 28:2

For Contemplative Action

Take a day to listen for words, phrases, and idioms we use in our everyday conversations. Look and listen to the marketing and advertising we are exposed to. Pay attention to the words you choose and the reactions you have to the world around you. Keep a log of the ways you experience the *habitus* of aggression. Become aware. As you experience the current *habitus*, identify how the dominant way of being can be disestablished by mercy. As you come up with counter-measures, write them in your log.

4

Diversity: The Key to Resilience

> We want our systems to look like us, think like us, believe like us, and behave like us. ~ Robert Putnam

Sometimes we are unaware of how diversity is necessary for life, deeply embedded not only in humanity but in natural systems and in the very fabric of the universe. Diversity makes life possible. It also makes life interesting. If every house on the block looked the same, if every restaurant served the same food, if everyone talked at us for hours about things we already knew, life just would not have much life at all.

Diversity makes whole systems possible: You need diverse parts to make a simple mechanical system like a bicycle or a complex mechanical system like a car. An ecosystem needs diverse species, consisting of complex food networks and cycles that keep the whole thing going. Our entire economic system, with all its different jobs, products, services, and forms of exchange, depends on diversity.

Diversity is the key to resilience. If all our corn is genetically identical, and a virulent bug attacks it, the entire crop may all be killed off. If our corn is genetically diverse, then some of it will succumb and some will survive. The surviving crop will reproduce, resulting in greater resistance to that bug. If everyone depends on one mega-corporation for a monopolized product ... if everyone uses the same operating system for their computers ... if all the production facilities use the single most efficient form of manufacturing ... if all the commuter trains are put out of business so all commuters must drive ... if we all get our electricity from a single grid with no distributed local energy sources, we make ourselves vulnerable to the collapse of the single item we all depend on. Many of us still remember the panic around Y2K. When the world's computers' clocks flipped time from the year 1999 to 2000, many predicted a programming glitch would bring central systems to a halt, triggering a catastrophic domino effect. Lack of technological diversity is a nightmare for terrorist emergency response planners who fear that terrorists could knock out a vital link in some system that we all depend on, for which there is no good alternative. If malware successfully infects just one machine on your computer network, it can attack every system on your network. Alternatives, and diversity are imperative to survival.

Among us humans, diversity is virtually infinite. Our diversity is a resource. We can tap our diverse strengths, skills, aptitudes, forms of intelligence, experiences in ways that make us much more powerful than we could ever be separately. This is a fundamental principle of modern social organization: Create a lot of diverse specialists, producers and consumers and then connect them up to exchange information, services and products.

In short, we need diversity. We thrive on diversity. We love diversity ... except when it comes to life in religious communities like churches. Some church growth experts will tell you if you really want to grow a church you must implement what they call the *homogeneous unit principal*, or *network homogeneity*: people like to be with people who are like them. Therefore, to grow your church, target people that are just like you. Build a comfort zone in the church that will not be threatened by racial, cultural, or socioeconomic diversity. Principles of homogeneity state, "We want our systems to look like us, think like us, believe like us, and behave like us." The challenge is that all those in the system share common vulnerabilities that can be exploited.

Thinking about diversity brings up two thorny issues. One is that too much diversity can have a negative effect on civic engagement. Robert Putnam, the social scientist of *Bowling Alone* fame, researched the effects of diversity on community life. As a self-professing liberal who favors diversity and multiculturalism, he came up with some surprising results. Putnam found that the greater the diversity in a community, the fewer people vote and the less they volunteer. The greater the diversity in a community, the less people give to charity and work on community projects. In the most diverse communities, neighbors trust one another about half as much as they do in settings where people are more alike. In more diverse communities, he says, there is a general civic malaise. Levels of trust are not only lower between groups in more diverse settings, but even among members of the same group. Putnam concluded inhabitants of diverse communities tend to withdraw from collective life; to distrust their neighbors, regardless of the color of their skin; withdraw even from close friends; expect the worst from their community and its leaders; volunteer less, give less to charity, and work on community projects less often; register to vote less; agitate for social reform more, but have less faith that they can actually make a difference; and huddle unhappily in front of the television. He wrote, "Diversity, at least in the short run, seems to bring out the turtle in all of us."[35]

If diversity tends to reduce social capital, spiritual activists invoke a different vision of humanity where we create a new and spacious sense of community. As Putnam says, we can reconstruct diversity in a way, "that does not bleach out ethnic specificities, but creates overarching identities that ensure that those specificities do not trigger the allergic, 'hunker down' reaction."[36] In other words, resilience can be found in *multi-relational* or *heterogeneous networks*

A second problematic issue is lack of diversity can lead to a fixation on purity. In extreme cases, a community will purify itself by eliminating all who are different. If you do not think this happens in churches, then you have forgotten those despicable preachers

---

35 Putnam, Robert D. "E Pluribus Unum: Diversity and Community in the Twenty-first Century," *Scandinavian Political Studies*, Vol. 30, No. 2 (2007), 150-151.
36 Putnam, 163-164.

who believe that all disasters in America are punishment for tolerating gays. Some faith leaders go as far as to say God hates all gay people. Fixating on purity comes from a belief that the source of evil lies outside of a person. We sometimes forget that evil also lives inside a person in an impure heart.[37]

One can easily be snared by the trap of false purity. Excluding "the other" happens when we become uncomfortable with anything that disturbs our identities or re-arranges our cultural norms. Eric Law, an Episcopal priest and director of the Kaleidoscope Institute, writes about the enormous number of words in the English language that we use describe exclusion: omission, segregation, apartheid, banishment, deletion, deportation, discrimination, elimination, exemption, expulsion, expurgation, rejection, and removal. We can ban, bar, blackball, blacklist, boycott, delete, drop, disregard, eject, excommunicate, expel, forbid, isolate, omit, ostracize, overlook, prohibit, reject, segregate, separate, shun, and shut out. Words like these represent "symbolic exclusion," or language and ideas that undergird segregation and often dehumanization of the other.

How many words do we should describe inclusion? If we are talking about the inclusion of people, we have, by comparison only a handful of words: accommodate, add, embody, embrace, encompass, incorporate, and involve.[38] Why is this the case? Law thinks one reason may be that exclusion is simple. Once we reject others, we do not have to deal with them anymore. No change. No hassle. No worries. Inclusion involves a great deal of thinking and listening. Inclusion requires time and energy. Inclusion requires change.

Spiritual activists work and pray to honor diversity within safe, positive, and nurturing environments. We desire to move beyond simple tolerance toward genuine understanding. We recognize that all people are free to make choices regarding their own personal and spiritual journeys. In short, we commit to build a variegated,

---

37 Miroslav Volf, *Exclusion and Embrace* (Nashville: Abingdon, 1996), 74-76.
38 Eric Law, *Inclusion: Making Room for Grace* (St. Louis: Chalice, 2000), 6.

loving community of faith because we believe God is committed to diversity. God loves to display the diversity of creation. God is so committed to diversity that God's own self is diverse too. Christians call it the doctrine of the Trinity. Diversity lies at the heart of God — distinct persons in a unity of love. Christian theology stumbles on the notion of God as a solitary, self-sufficient monarch who issues commandments that must be obeyed. If God is Trinity, God's being is community and the different persons are dependent on one another. To honor the diversity in operation within God's unity, our religious traditions use multi-lingual frameworks for God. When we become stuck with just one image, or one word for God, the concept of the Trinity helps shake us out of that sludge and offers us a variety of ways to address and experience the Divine.

For Conversation

While the word "diverse" can mean "varied," it also comes with a negative etymological meaning: "being contrary to what is agreeable or right." While diversity is held up as a virtue in modern times, the concept is sensed by many to be a threat. What does the word "diversity" evoke in you?

Tell a story about a time when you saw it as a strength that people in your community were different from one another. "Differences" can include racial or ethnic differences; political, theological or lifestyle differences; family differences; or socio-economic differences.

Do you think everyone in your faith community thinks the same way about God? Politics? How to raise a family? Economics? Is it OK when people do not agree on important values? Why or why not?

For Active Contemplation

Have you ever felt uncomfortable in your faith community because of another person's presence? What made you uncomfortable? How did the situation resolve? Once you have a situation in mind, take time, through prayer and meditation, to imagine a different conclusion or alternative narrative. If you had to face the same situation again, would you do anything differently? How might you engage that uncomfortable situation in a way that brings out the best of who you are?

In a group, ask participants to do a five-minute free write based on two prompts: (1) Recall a time from your faith experience when you felt especially included, engaged, appreciated, and validated in a faith community. (2) Recall a situation when you felt especially excluded, alienated, and invalidated in a faith community. In small groups, ask participants to share the parts of their stories they feel comfortable sharing. Once everybody shares both stories, ask them to reflect upon the similarities and differences in their stories. This activity can provide grist for faith leaders and group facilitators to reexamine their own practices. As a conversation point, the group can talk about ways the community unintentionally alienates or excludes its members.

FOR CONTEMPLATIVE ACTION

Quick Decisions is a classic nonviolent training tool.[39] In one minute, groups are challenged to reach a decision of an action to take based on some situation. First, get participants into small groups (4 to 8 people, depending on the size of the overall group). Explain that participants are going to get a chance to make very quick decisions as a team. In a matter of minutes, the team needs to reach a decision quickly, based on a particular scenario.

After reading the first scenario out loud, time the teams as they reach a decision. After time is up, get the result each group reached (or did not reach). Debrief a little after each scenario. Debriefing can happen at two levels: decision-making process and then the quality of the decision and its implications. Make sure to keep the debrief moving. Here are some scenarios to consider:

---

39 Virginia Coover, et al., *Resource Manual for a Living Revolution* (British Columbia: New Society Press: 1978), 59-61.

A trusted church member calls the pastor and asks that a stranger who needs emergency housing be allowed to sleep at the church for a night. Do you allow it?

A vandal spray paints a racial epithet on the side of your house of worship after your church takes a public anti-racism stand. Do you continue your stand? Why or why not?

Your congregation shares its space with another congregation from a different ethnic and worship culture. Members of the other congregation use some of your sacred objects without asking. After repeated request for them to stop, the other congregation persists in their behavior and members of your congregation are getting angry. How do you respond?

A member with severe mental illness comes to worship and threatens violence. While people have overlooked these episodes in the past, this time it feels dangerous. How do you respond?

Suggested Debriefing Questions:

- Does your option give you more time to respond?
- How does your decision impact your team's perception of inclusion?
- Where is your group's sense of security coming from at this moment? How does your action increase or decrease your safety?

5

DISMANTLING RACISM

It is an unhappy truth that racism is a way of life for the vast majority of white Americans, spoken and unspoken, acknowledged and denied, subtle and sometimes not so subtle--the disease of racism permeates and poisons a whole body politic. And I can see nothing more urgent than for America to work passionately and unrelentingly — to get rid of the disease of racism ... I submit that nothing will be done until people of goodwill put their bodies and their souls in motion ... We're going to win our freedom because both the sacred heritage of our nation and the eternal will of the almighty God are embodied in our echoing demands. And so, however dark it is, however deep the angry feelings are, and however violent [the] explosions are, I can still sing 'We Shall Overcome.' We shall overcome because the arc of the moral universe is long, but it bends toward justice.[40]
~ Rev. Dr. Martin Luther King, Jr.

In September 2015, addressing a joint session of Congress, Pope Francis challenged the American Dream and our county's ongoing challenges with racism. Pope Francis said, "A nation can be considered great when it . . . fosters a culture which enables people to 'dream' of full rights for all their brothers and sisters, as

---

[40] Martin Luther King, Jr., "Remaining Awake Through a Great Revolution," *King Encyclopedia* (April 9, 1968), http://mlk-kpp01.stanford.edu/index.php/encyclopedia/documentsentry/doc_remaining_awake_through_a_great_revolution.

Martin Luther King sought to do."[41] Dr. King's dream provided a radical, non-violent counterpoint to the racial and socioeconomic inequality in our country. Is Dr. King's dream realized? Yes, society has made gains. Yes, our awareness has grown and there is no turning back. Yes, people of goodwill *have* put their bodies and souls in motion. But, have we overcome? Is the "eternal will of almighty God" still heard in our demands for equality?

Let's not spend time arguing about whether racism still exists in America today. Here is this book's assumption: Racism still exists, and it is the job of the spiritual activist to confront it, condemn it, and close it down. For African Americans, for people of Latin American descent (hereafter referred to as Latinx), for Native and Asian Americans, for other non-white ethnicities, the dream of true equality is taking too long to come true. We have been dreaming about a world of true equality for a long, long time. Christians have supposedly been aiming for this dream since the Apostle Paul first taught about God's realm where there is no Jew or Greek, no slave or free, and where all are united in the love of God.[42] We have taken steps towards it, but that dream is not yet fulfilled.

Humans can be creatures of duality who speak a language of color-coded values. In his book, *Uprooting Racism*, Paul Kivel explains how whiteness has defined our culture for hundreds of years — so much so that it makes its way into our language and our values. Embedded in our language is the idea that the color white and the people associated with it are good. Dark colors, and those connected with them are dangerous, threatening or manipulative. Consider the following list of words and phrases: black deed, black list, black market, black-hearted, blackmail, black sheep, black magic, black death, black mark, black mood, black with rage, dark ages, the dark side, to be in the dark, yellow bellied, yellow peril, red

---

41   Pope Francis. "Transcript: Pope Francis's speech to Congress," *The Washington Post* (Sept. 24, 2015), https://www.washingtonpost.com/local/social-issues/transcript-pope-franciss-speech-to-congress/2015/09/24/6d7d7ac8-62bf-11e5-8e9e-dce8a2a2a679_story.html?utm_term=.695b917ce211.

42   See Galatians 3:28

menace, redskin, great white hope, white knight, whitewash, white wedding, pure/white as snow.[43] Take a moment to notice the idioms we use. Notice how a dualism between white and black, light and dark, good and bad, is embedded in white culture. When we become aware, we can continue to look for ways to communicate that are not only respectful, but run counter to centuries of white exploitation and domination.

Even doing something as small as noticing our idioms feels like hard work. What might happen if we looked hard at our social relationships? A recent study by Public Religion Research Institute showed three quarters of Whites do not have any Black friends. In a 100-friend scenario, the average White person has 91 white friends; 1 each of Black, Latinx, Asian, mixed race, and other races; and 3 friends of unknown race. The average Black person, on the other hand, has 83 Black friends, 8 White friends, 2 Latinx friends, zero Asian friends, 3 mixed race friends, 1 other race friend and four friends of unknown race. One chief obstacle to having an intelligent conversation across the racial divide is that White Americans with means tend to self-segregate. They talk mostly to other White people and may choose to live in communities that face far fewer race-related problems.[44]

Condemning racism, on macro levels, is the integrative work of spiritual activism. However, before we dismantle racism on the macro-level, some researchers contend that we should work on the smallest effective level first. Spiritual activists can begin by reflecting on their friendship history through a racial lens. Spiritual activists can also seek out ways to develop personal and professional diversity competencies and emotional resilience. That is, we know when we take the courageous step to engage in mutual conversations

---

43   Paul Kivel, *Uprooting Racism: How White People Can Work for Racial Justice* (Philadelphia, PA: New Society Publishers, 1995).
44   Robert Jones, "Self-Segregation: Why It's So Hard for Whites to Understand Ferguson." *The Atlantic* (August 21, 2014), http://www.theatlantic.com/national/archive/2014/08/self-segregation-why-its-hard-for-whites-to-understand-ferguson/378928/.

about race and racism, we will make mistakes. Learn from them. Breathe, listen, and then try again.[45]

When we listen to the pain of others, we open ourselves to the suffering love of God. When we address injustice in the world actively, we can help heal the world. This is a significant point for religious liberals and humanists who tend to dismiss healing as a central part of religion. Part of the function of religion is to heal our souls when we are damaged by the injustice of the world.

So, the question is not whether racism exists. The question is, how are we going to transform our communities? Are religious traditions helping to confront systems of domination? To answer this question, we need to gain clarity on the hoped-for outcomes of dismantling racism. There are different approaches with different goals and worldviews. An anti-racism worldview says, "The world is controlled by powerful systems with historically traceable roots. Once people are shown how they benefit from or are battered by those systems, they can work together to change the systems." The hoped-for outcome is to bring about social change.

Others dismantle racism by constructing multi-cultural institutions. The diversity-and-multiculturalism worldview differs from the anti-racism stance. Multiculturalism says, "The world is filled with a multitude of complex cultures, constantly intersecting and shaping each other. As people grow to understand and appreciate their own culture and cultures around them, they will be better able to cooperate and overcome mutual problems." The hoped-for outcome is tolerance and awareness of cultural differences.

We could also talk about dismantling racism through a process of truth and reconciliation. A reconciliation worldview says, "The world is filled with groups that have been traumatized and victimized by historic events. When the oppressing group acknowledges and apologizes for these injustices, individual and social healing,

---

45 See Deborah Plummer, *Racing Across the Lines: Changing Race Relations Through Friendship* (Cleveland: Pilgrim Press, 2004).

reconciliation and change can occur." The hoped-for outcome is individual transformation.[46]

No single one of these is better than the other. They have some overlapping concepts and goals. When all is said and processed, the task of the spiritual activist is to invest in relationships, to listen to one another with reverence, to speak from the heart, to deal with conflict, and to honor all people. If we want to be spiritual activists who address society's problems with contemplative action, we need to confront racism on systemic, institutional, and individual levels. Because, for all the work we have done, racism lurks everywhere.

According to the 2010 census, 26.6% of all Hispanic persons (of any race) and 27.4% of all Black persons are living in poverty.[47] If we want to be spiritual activists who begin to end poverty, then we begin with ending the poverty of racism.

Even though incarceration rates among Black males have decreased sizeable since 2000, there is still a substantial racial disparity between Blacks and Whites in prison. Black men are incarcerated at a rate 5 times higher than White males.[48] There are over 2.5 times as many Hispanics in jail as Whites. Many African Americans and Hispanics are less able to afford high quality legal services and they may be subject to discrimination in prosecution and sentencing. Some prosecutors have made a practice of eliminating Blacks from their prospective juries, increasing the likelihood of a race-based decision.[49] If we want to be spiritual activists who address the injustice of the penal system, we also need to address the injustices of racism.

---

46 Ilana Shapiro, "A Guide to Selected Programs for Racial Equity Inclusion" (2002), http://www.aspeninstitute.org/sites/default/files/content/docs/rcc/training.pdf.
47 2010 Census, http://www.census.gov/2010census/.
48 Keith Humphreys, "There's been a big decline in the black incarceration rate, and almost nobody's paying attention," *Washington Post* (Feb. 10, 2016), https://www.washingtonpost.com/news/wonk/wp/2016/02/10/almost-nobody-is-paying-attention-to-this-massive-change-in-criminal-justice/?utm_term=.cccd24274e5f.
49 "Factoid: Black Male Incarceration Rate Is 6 Times Greater Than Rate for White Males" (November 3, 2009), http://allotherpersons.wordpress.

African American women who have college degrees, who have insurance, and who have good jobs have higher rates of infant mortality than White women who dropped out of school after eighth grade, who do not have high occupational status, and who do not have very good health care. Why is this? African Americans routinely get less access to health care and less quality care. Some research indicates that racism generates a physiological affect that overloads the body. Affluent or middle-class African-American women experience so much daily stress from racism, their bodies cannot rest. Their blood pressure stays elevated at night. Their immune systems become compromised. Racism and discrimination are a public health matter.[50] If we want to be spiritual activists who heal our nation's public health crisis, we also need to heal the disease of racism.

During the sub-prime mortgage crisis, data from the 100 largest U.S. metropolitan areas found that living in a predominantly African-American area, and to a lesser extent Hispanic area, predicted foreclosures across the nation. Predatory lending aimed at racially segregated minority neighborhoods led to mass foreclosures that fueled the U.S. housing crisis.[51] If we want to help construct housing markets where all people in this land have a suitable roof over their heads, then we also need to deconstruct racism.

If we are going to talk about poverty and housing, then we need to talk about the environment to which they are linked. In the United States, lead poisoning continues to be the number one environmental health threat to children living in inner cities. Nationally, three out of five African Americans and Latinx Americans live in communities with abandoned toxic waste sites. Some predict

---

com/2009/11/03/factoid-black-male-incarceration-rate-is-6-times-greater-than-rate-for-white-males/.

50 Barnes-Josiah, Debora, "Undoing Racism in Public Health: A Blueprint for Action in Urban MCH (August 1, 2004), http://webmedia.unmc.edu/Community/CityMatch/CityMatCHUndoingRacismReport.pdf.

51 "Racial Predatory Loans Fueled U.S. Housing Crisis: Study" (Reuters, October 4, 2010), http://www.reuters.com/article/2010/10/04/us-usa-foreclosures-race-idUSTRE6930K520101004.

climate change will negatively affect poor American families who will have to spend even more on food and electricity, which already represent a large portion of their budgets. In 1987, the Commission for Racial Justice of the United Church of Christ coined the term *environmental racism*, defined as corporate and government actions that result in the unequal exposure of people of color and low-income people to environmental dangers that threaten their physical, social, economic, or environmental health and well-being. The Commission found a link between a person's race and one's likelihood of living near a hazardous waste facility. Evidence mounted quickly, alleging that people of color and low-income communities bear a lop-sided share of environmental dangers and thus are victims of environmental racism. In some cases, race is a more significant indicator of pollution burdens than income, poverty, childhood poverty, education, employment or home ownership.[52] If we want to be spiritual activists who care for the earth and its people, then we must eradicate toxic racism that poisons our communities.

What about our schools? Institutional racism is subtle, and often unintentional, but always potent. Many students of color do not have access to fully credentialed teachers or high-quality curriculum materials and advanced courses. The Southern Poverty Law Center reviewed civil rights history programs in standards across the country and found that most states get a failing grade. 16 states do not require any instruction about the civil rights movement. In another 19, coverage is minimal.[53] If we, as spiritual activists, want to solve our education crisis, then we also need to dissolve racism.

---

52 "Environmental Racism," United Church of Christ, http://www.ucc.org/environmental-ministries_environmental-racism. See also, Mike Ewall, "Legal Tools for Environmental Equity vs. Environmental Justice" (October 15, 2012), http://www.ejnet.org/ej/ejlaw.pdf.
53 "SPLC Study Finds That More Than Half of States Fail at Teaching the Civil Rights Movement." Southern Poverty Law Center, https://www.splcenter.org/news/2011/09/28/splc-study-finds-more-half-states-fail-teaching-civil-rights-movement.

Dr. King knew that it was not up to God to deliver anyone from racism. Dr. King might say that we cannot wait for miracles. We must march forward and seize them. He might say that the Reign of God will come in its fullness as soon as we open our eyes and truly see the many difficulties around us and the real challenges that come with awareness. We refuse to gloss over history but see the pain and hear the suffering of others. We seek to live not in a melting pot where all is formless and void, but in a place where our stories and languages and cultures are valued and where our wounds are healed by repentance. We strive to know and respect our differences and make possible the highest expectations for humanity. We do the work of liberating ourselves from hatred, beginning in the modest places of our longing souls. And, we always reach out, with our words, our actions, our prayers, our love, and our hands, to all souls. *All* souls. This is how the world can be made whole again and its entire people one.

For Conversation

Some congregations engage in anti-racism audits of their worship and ministries. Here are some questions to consider:

- How often are members of racial/ethnic groups not of the majority included in leadership in your faith community? How might you include them if you are not doing so on a regular basis?
- How often do you actively pray to overcome racism and social injustice during regular worship services?
- What educational experiences do you offer to deal with issues of racism and cultural diversity? Does your curriculum include stories and images of people of color?
- What small steps could we take immediately to be more inclusive of all groups?
- Where do we want our faith community to be in relation to this work a year from now? Where do we want to be five years from now?

The Space Between 47

- How can we begin to address some of the larger manifestations of racism in our faith community and in the world?

FOR ACTIVE CONTEMPLATION

Artists like Janet McKenzie, Fr. John Giuliani, Fr. Robert Lenz are Roman Catholics who create iconographic images of Christian Saints and devotional figures in the style of the Eastern Orthodox Church. Like all icons, the pictures are not there just to be looked at; they are spiritual portraits that speak a multi-sensory language. When we pray with icons, we engage not only the mind, but the whole person — body, mind, and spirit. As iconographer Linette Martin writes,

> As we move toward an icon, it moves toward us with a warm and precise Christian content if we understand the language that it speaks. The primary purpose of an icon is to enable a face-to-face encounter with a holy person or make present a sacred event. Icons are also "theology in color."[54]

McKenzie, Lenz, and Giuliani, as well as other artists, have several icons that depict a non-White Jesus. Prayerfully reflect on these, or similar images as an individual or in a group. What prayers do they invoke in you? How do the images open you to a wider understanding of the Holy? When you pray with these images, where in your body do you sense them speaking?

- *Jesus of the People*: http://www.bridgebuilding.com/narr/jmjep.html. Jesus of the People won the National Catholic Reporter Jesus 2000 competition, which sought a powerful portrayal of Christ at the millennium, drew nearly 1,700 other entries from around the world.
- *Christ in Ascension:* http://www.bridgebuilding.com/narr/gasc.html. Jesus is imaged in the features of America's indigenous peoples. It celebrates the soul of the Native American as the original spiritual presence on this continent, and celebrates the

---

54 Martin, Lynette, *Sacred Doorways: A Beginners Guide to Icons* (Brewster, MA: Paraclete Press, 1997), xv.

reconciliation of the spiritual vision of Native and Christian peoples of this land.
- *Jesus Christ, Liberator:* http://robertlentz.com/selected-works/. This image depicts Christ's solidarity with the Black peoples of the world.
- *Compassion Mandala:* https://www.trinitystores.com/store/art-image/compassion-mandala. A figure sits within a sacred mandala, a representation of the cosmos, encompassing the world in arms of love.
- *Christ appears to Mary*: http://www.jesusmafa.com. Not an icon, but a painting, this is a response to the New Testament readings from the Lectionary by a Christian community in Cameroon, Africa.
- *Jesus* by Lois Glanzman: http://www.louisglanzman.com/jesus.html. Not the Caucasian Jesus many of us are used to seeing.
- *Good Shepherd:* http://www.cnn.com/SPECIALS/1999/china.50/dispatches/09.20.spirituality/good.shepherd.jpg. Shanghai-based artist Yu Jiade's interpretation of Jesus as a Chinese man.

For Contemplative Action

Consider reading and convening a study group or sacred conversation on systemic racism in the United States. Some resources to consider:

- *The New Jim Crow: Mass Incarceration in the Age of Colorblindness* by Michelle Alexander (The New Press: 2012). Alexander explores how mass incarceration is the new form of explicit racial segregation in the United States.
- "The Case for Reparations" by Ta-Nehisi Coates in *Atlantic Monthly* (June 2014), accessible at http://www.theatlantic.com/magazine/archive/2014/06/the-case-for-reparations/361631. Coates explains the devastating effects of housing discrimination on African-American communities

and makes a case for reparations to those who have been disaffected.
- *White Awareness: Handbook for Anti-Racism Training* by Judith H. Katz (University of Oklahoma Press: 2003). This training program provides a meaningful way to help dismantle racism in the White community.
- *Uprooting Racism: How White People Can Work for Racial Justice* by Paul Kivel (New Society Publishers: 2011). Kivel offers a framework for understanding institutional racism. He also includes information about specific cultural groups such as Muslims, people with mixed-heritage, Native Americans, Jews, recent immigrants, Asian Americans, and Latinos.

6

Compassion Is an Act of Resistance

> …kindness is resistance. Truth is resistance. Wisdom is resistance. Compassion is resistance. Hope is resistance.
> ~ A Tweet by Rachel Held Evans

> To have compassion we must believe in the ultimate goodness of human nature … We have to decide to love above all else — above our egos and pride, above our own fears and insecurities, and above our own hatred and hostility. We must fight the urge to lash out, even when there are truly legitimate reasons to do so.
> ~ Damsels in Defiance[55]

"Resist!" The imperative is plastered all over my Facebook feed and echoed in the voices of my friends, congregants, and denominational leaders. At a moment in our national life when the political landscape appears to be crumbling into authoritarianism, we are called to resist more than ever. When hard-fought civil rights are on the line — rights we hoped were set in cement, which are corroded with each new executive order from the White House — people in my faith community respond with our voice and with our feet. We march, we protest, we demonstrate, we call our representatives, and we shout in solidarity with those whose power is diminished. This is what democracy looks like!

---

55 "What is Compassionate Resistance?" *Damsels in Defiance*, https://damselsindefiance.org/what-is-compassionate-resistance/.

I am all for acts of public resistance against those who seek to solidify their authority by obstructing the rights of others. We must speak truth to power. I also heed the warnings of both our historical political commentators and our spiritual ancestors: revolt and resistance that serve the motive of the individual ego can lead to violence and set up the resistors to become tyrants themselves. Today's revolutionaries may become tomorrow's dictators. As Albert Camus reminds us in *The Rebel*,

> we understand that rebellion cannot exist without a strange form of love. Those who find no rest in God or in history are condemned to live for those who, like themselves, cannot live: in fact, for the humiliated. The most pure form of the movement of rebellion is thus crowned with the heart-rending cry of Karamazov: if all are not saved, what good is the salvation of one only?[56]

Only when resistance springs from a commitment to the salvation of the other are the most courageous acts of solidarity born. In *The Compassionate Life*, His Holiness the Dalai Lama helps us understand the nature of other-centered resistance instead of ego-centered resistance.

> Genuine compassion is based not on our own projections and expectations, but rather on the needs of the other: irrespective of whether another person is a close friend or an enemy, as long as that person wishes for peace and happiness and wishes to overcome suffering, then on that basis we develop genuine concern for their problem. This is genuine compassion.[57]

Ego-driven resistance feeds polarization. Other-driven resistance disarms it.

I have learned something very important in my years of ministry. There is a difference between pity and compassion. Showing

---

56 Albert Camus, *The Rebel: An Essay on Man in Revolt*, Anthony Bower, trans (New York: Vintage International, 1956), 301.

57 Tenzin Gayatso, the Fourteenth Dalai Lama, *The Compassionate Life* (Boston: Wisdom, 2003), 21.

pity is about me. Pity is when I do something to someone that makes me feel better. Pity saves me. Compassion is about the other. It is what happens when we share our power to forge a more loving and more just world. Compassion saves us all.

Can I show compassion without condition or restraint, even if it means being taken advantage of? Even if it means giving of that which I value? I confess, those are difficult questions for me to answer. I have a deep fear right now. I must resist the enemies I make in my own heart if I want to resist the hate in the world. I must resist violence without becoming violent. I must resist the ceaseless din of division by re-connecting and listening deeply, on the most local level, to the voices of struggle and pain in my community.

We must show compassion courageously.

Courageous Compassion means loving everyone; touching pain without first mapping out the consequences; embodying love in action to those who offend us, to those who have hurt us, and to those who do not deserve a second chance (or a third or fourth); turning the status quo upside down with a commitment to love; confronting unjust family systems, religious systems, and economic or political systems that offer great gifts to insiders while pushing others to the side. In the Spirit's Reign, there are no insiders and no outsiders. We are all one nature, one flesh, one grief, and one hope. If we fail to love, we fail in everything else.

I am training my heart to listen to people at the grocery store, at the gas station, at the gym, at the office, in the neighborhood, and the people I see as I am stuck in Washington, D.C. traffic. I will give myself permission to be inconvenienced by their pains. I will let myself be moved by compassion that is free from any strings. Who knows, these small acts of other-centered love might just feed an uprising of peace when each of us becomes engaged compassionately in our community and our world.

COMPASSION IS OUR COMPASS

Years ago, someone asked the great anthropologist Margaret Mead, "What is the sign of civilization that you have discovered that gives light and life to a culture?" The person who asked the question thought maybe she would say, "Well, it was when we discovered a clay pot that someone formed and molded." Another would have thought, "Well, maybe it was a fish hook. That's when civilization took hold, or maybe a grinding stone, an example of a larger way to be fed."

Dr. Mead said something that took everyone off-guard. The first sign of civilization that she knew anything about was a healed femur. That is the big bone that sits above the knee. When archaeologists discovered a person whose femur had healed, she realized that someone else had taken care of that person, that the individual could no longer hunt or gather, and so someone else had to do those things for this person. It represented the burgeoning of compassion in civilization. Compassion is the evidence that a society is becoming a civilization.

Compassion literally means to suffer with another. Compassion is what begins to identify us as sophisticated creatures. Compassion directs to our lives. Compassion is our compass. And compassion is in short supply. I have noticed that some people seem to think that compassion should be qualified. Conditional Compassion is an American way of thinking. We have been taught there are limits to compassion — only those who deserve help should get my attention. Consider how the term "deserving poor" enters debates about welfare and entitlement benefits. The word "deserving" masks an ugly philosophy, an idea that certain people (and certain people only) earn whatever happens to them. This attitude is ultimately based on nothing more than irrational double standards. The undeserving poor are those who are poor through no fault of their own, either because of illness, accident or age, or because there is no work available for them. The deserving poor are perceived to be poor because of laziness or personal problems like addiction. American society decided that the deserving poor do not deserve much help. We are told that we must be willing to step away and let those who have dug their own hole suffer the consequences of their wrongdoing.[58]

Dualities like deserving and undeserving lead to questions about entitlement and rights. Are both the deserving and undeserving entitled to medical care? Should both the deserving and undeserving get food and shelter for their children? Do both the deserving and undeserving have a right to experience well-being and safety? Are we entitled to find work, or to earn money and to keep the profits we earn? Only when we learn to manage this balance between our own needs and those of others can we have genuine, satisfying, and intimate relationships with other people. Only when our compassion points us to rethink who is in and who is out, who gets care and who does not, only then do we begin to find our way.

The Chinese are among the first people to have a recorded history of using a compass for navigation on land and on sea. These first compasses relied on a natural magnet, a lodestone, to point in a consistent direction to set one's bearings. The Chinese words for lodestone literally mean "loving stone." The French word for magnet also means loving. Love has the power of attraction. Our compass of compassion is a magnetic force that guides us through the influence of attraction along the path of love. We should never have to decide whether someone is worthy of our compassion. Compassion is too important for that. Compassion is our compass. Compassion points us in the right direction when it is offered unconditionally and without judgment.

For Conversation

- Why is it important to show compassion towards those we dislike?

---

58 Kristina Cooke, David Rhode, Ryan McNeil, "The Undeserving Poor," *The Atlantic* (Dec. 20, 2012), https://www.theatlantic.com/busines s/archive/2012/12/the-undeserving-poor/266507/.

- What does your faith tradition say about compassion?
- Is there a disadvantage to being caring and compassionate when it comes to social activism?

For Active Contemplation

A key to compassionate resistance is the prayerful realization that we are not so different from our enemies. We are all a few decisions away from making the same kinds of decisions as those we try to resist. We ask God to support, forgive, and comfort us as we stand against all that seeks to destroy our beleaguered planet and its people. In your personal devotional time, consider these words of Anselm, (c. 1033-1109), a monk, pastor, and ultimately archbishop of Canterbury. Like most faith leaders, he had several enemies. He prayed,

> *Tender Lord Jesus,*
> *let me not be the cause of the death of my brothers and sisters,*
> *let me not be to them*
> *a stone of stumbling and a rock of offence.*
> *For it is more than enough, Lord,*
> *that I should be a scandal to myself,*
> *my sin is sufficient to me.*
>
> *Your slave begs you for his fellow slaves,*
> *lest because of me they offend*
> *against the kindness of so good and great a lord.*
> *Let them be reconciled to you and in concord with me,*
> *according to your will and for your own sake.*[59]

For Contemplative Action

Compassion is not just an idea. It is concrete. It is love in action, especially on the side of the oppressed. Liberation theolo-

---

[59] Posted by Julia Marks on *The Value of Sparrows: Writings of a Christian Mystic*, https://thevalueofsparrows.com/2012/11/12/prayer-a-prayer-for-friends-and-a-prayer-for-enemies-by-anselm/.

gians remind us that even our enemies and oppressors will also be set free as we love the oppressed. Liberating the poor shows love to both the oppressed and the oppressor. Love identified with justice does not equate itself with compromise or acceptance of evil. It is a love that condemns acts of evil. Compassionate love becomes one of the guiding principles in forging a new society.[60] Find a direct, non-violent action in your area and have members of your faith community participate. If this is not something your congregation is used to doing, make sure to gather prayerfully both before and after the event to consider how your engagement informs your faith and how faith informs your engagement.

---

60 Linda H. Damico, The *Anarchist Dimension of Liberation Theology* (Eugene, OR: Wipf & Stock, 1989), 58-59.

7

Double Justice

*Justice, and only justice,
you shall pursue, so that you may
live and occupy the land that the Lord your
God is giving you.
~ Deuteronomy 16:20*

January 4, 2012. Headline: "Mother asks police to arrest her squabbling children." When police arrived, the mother lamented that her five children were fighting all day. The mother could not stand the bickering, so she went out for a while to run a few errands. While she was away, her son, a 15-year-old, punched his 8-year-old sister in the arm. That provoked an intervention from the older 16-year-old daughter, trying to protect her sister. When asked what she felt the Police Department could do to assist her with the issues she's having as a parent, the mother replied, "I want them both out of here." According to the report, she then asked to have the older brother and sister arrested.[61] This is a complicated little story. On one hand, what parent, after listening to a child tattle on a sibling for breathing, does not want to send the "little angels" away for a day? Everyone needs a little break now and then. On the other hand, conflict can escalate so high that, if not stopped, it can have disastrous consequences. How will the children respond to their mother from now on? Does the mother regret her decision to ask for the arrest her children? Will this family be able

---

61 Alan Burke, "Police: Mother Asks Officers to Arrest Her Squabbling Children," *The Salem News* (January 12, 2012), http://www.salemnews.com/local/x191087269/Police-Mother-asks-officers-to-arrest-her-squabbling-children.

to forgive, or will they instinctively seek revenge against each other? Will anyone get justice?

Unfortunately, when some people talk about justice, they mean vengeance, punishment, pain for pain, and an eye for an eye. Some people become impatient with any delays in the gratification that comes from revenge.

Some Christians have a theological rationale for revenge. The argument goes something like this: Since God is holy and perfect, God cannot tolerate sin. If sin contacts God, God must destroy it. Because of this holiness, God is not free to act with unconditional mercy and compassion toward rebellious human beings.[62]

Retributive theology may project our own vengeful impulses onto an image of God. In real life, when we are hurt, we want to hurt our enemy worse than they hurt us. Motivated by neither the common good nor the upholding of justice and truth, we simply want to get rid of our own pain by seeing ourselves as holy and perfect and our enemies punished for their evil behavior. Part of what makes us human is that we are not above taking revenge and bearing a grudge. Justice, in this framework, requires payment for wrong-doing. Let's call it the *dance of double exclusion*. In the first move of the dance of double exclusion, victims cry for justice. Their bonfires of rage burn against their perpetrators, inflamed by unredeemed suffering. The second step in the dance of double exclusion happens when the victim's sense of justice seeks revenge. It would be unjust to forgive. In the dance of double exclusion, a person can be both a perpetrator and a victim. Both the perpetrator and a victim are locked in footsteps of mutual exclusion and united in a knot of mutual hate.[63]

Forgiveness flounders when victims feel free to commit the same crimes that victimized them — when victims want justice for themselves while dehumanizing their enemy. The dance of double exclusion plunges victims into a descent of proud purity where

---

62 Ted Grimsrud, "Healing Justice: A Sermon," *Peace Theology* (January 18, 2009), http://peacetheology.net/pacifism/healing-justice-a-sermon/.
63 Hirschfield, 64-65, 68, 92.

they may forget that we are all human, that we are all sinful, and that we all answer to faith's call to repair the world. In a more forgiving world, we would realize that the people who hurt us have often been hurt themselves. We would remember that those against whom we struggle are actually "us," not some impersonal "them."

The counter-move to double exclusion is double justice. The idea comes from the Hebrew Scriptures. Deuteronomy 16 summons Israel to appoint judges and officials who will govern the tribes with due justice. The Law of Moses insists that justice is an eternal religious obligation. We hear it in Deuteronomy 16:20: "Justice, Justice, shall you pursue." Jewish scholars have long wondered why the word "justice" is repeated twice. Are the words paired for poetic emphasis, or is there more to it?

What if the repetition is intentional? What if the God of Israel expects people to work for double justice instead of double exclusion? Double justice means both victims and victimizers get treated fairly. If we want to stop rounds of revenge and reprisal, if we wish for marginalization and exploitation to end, if we seek to stop perpetrators from claiming victimhood, then spiritual activists must offer double justice. Yes, victims get compassionate justice, but not at the expense of dehumanizing the foe. Our spiritual traditions are quite clear: our enemies get compassionate justice, too.

Double exclusion means that I only get justice when my enemies are obliterated. Double justice means that my enemies get fair and humane treatment under the law. Double exclusion means that when I wish harm on my enemy, I sacrifice part of my own humanity. Double justice means that I seek fairness for the oppressor and the oppressed.

Most U.S. Marines know the story of the battle of Iwo Jima. U.S. Soldiers knew that the ancient Japanese warrior code did not believe in surrender, or being taken as prisoners. During the battle, some U.S. Marines began to retaliate with the killing of wounded, captured, or surrendering Japanese soldiers. One day, while on patrol, Dr. Robert Humphrey and his men came upon a young, emaciated Japanese soldier in a torn, filthy uniform. The young

Japanese soldier stood at the mouth of a cave, waving a white flag. It looked unusual. At the time, many believed Japanese troops faked surrender to kill Allied troops, often with a concealed grenade. Convinced that this was a trick, a Marine raised his rifle to kill the young man. Humphrey ordered the Marine to put down his weapon. Humphrey confronted the Marine, briefly but intensely. Order and discipline prevailed, and the Marine lowered his weapon. The Japanese soldier's surrender was genuine. Soldiers took him safely to the rear. The prisoner even turned out to be of some intelligence value.

Humphrey thought little of the incident at the time. There was so much killing before the incident, and so much afterward. Yet nearly fifty years later, when asked to share his proudest achievement, he cited this incident. He said, "On Iwo Jima, it was life or death every minute of every day. There was unavoidable killing every day. When I saw that Japanese boy trying to surrender and understood that this was perhaps the only time that I didn't have to kill, I took the opportunity. I believe that action saved my humanity."[64]

"Justice, Justice, shall you pursue." Only double justice will save humanity from itself. We protect the humanity of all people, even our enemies, even those we have been taught to fear, even those we have been taught to hate. Spiritual activists look for opportunities to practice double justice. No spiritual activist can be comfortable if there is a demon of vengeance in our communities of faith. No spiritual activist can be comfortable if there is emptiness of spirit or bareness of soul among us. No spiritual activist can be comfortable if there is injustice and inequality in our world. No spiritual activist can be a worker for justice if one's enemies are treated unfairly. The work of justice can be achieved, but true

---

64 Jack E. Hoban, Bruce J. Gourlie, "The Ethical Warrior: Protecting Our Enemies," *PoliceOne* (December 19, 2011), http://www.policeone.com/close-quarters-combat/articles/4836574-The-ethical-warrior-Protecting-our-enemies/.

justice is double justice; a power for life, a power for salvation, a power for love, a power for peace.

For Conversation

- Read this statement out loud: "Jesus loves haters, terrorists, murderers, and criminals." How does this statement make you feel? In what ways do you agree or disagree?
- In your own life or even the life of your community, or the nation, can you recall a time when an enemy became a friend? What paved the way to reconciliation?
- How can we love people who do not value us or who, at least, do not seem to?
- What does it mean to love people whom we do not know personally? What forms might such love assume?

For Active Contemplation

In his book Loving Our Enemies: Reflections on the Hardest Commandment, author Jim Forest writes,

> "If I cannot find the face of Jesus in the face of those whom I regard as enemies, if I cannot find him in the unbeautiful and damaged, if I cannot find him in those who have the 'wrong ideas,' if I cannot find him in the poor and the defeated and damaged, then how will I find him in bread and wine or in the life after death? If I do not reach out in this world to those with whom he has identified, why do I imagine that I will want to be with him, and them, in heaven? Why would I want to be for all eternity in the company of those I avoided every day of my life?"[65]

The monk, theologian and activist Thomas Merton once wrote these words:

> "Do not be too quick to assume that your enemy is an enemy of God just because he is your enemy. Perhaps he is your

---

[65] Jim Forest, *Loving Our Enemies: Reflections on the Hardest Commandment* (Maryknoll, NY: Orbis Press, 2014), 165.

enemy precisely because he can find nothing in you that gives glory to God. Perhaps he fears you because he can find nothing in you of God's love and God's kindness and God's patience and mercy and understanding of the weakness of men. Do not be too quick to condemn the man who no longer believes in God. For it is perhaps your own coldness and avarice and mediocrity and materialism and sensuality and selfishness that have killed his faith"[66]

- How can you include the ethos of these two quotes into your prayer life today? Do they evoke a prayer of confession? A gesture of release? A cry of the heart?
- What insight does the Spirit have for you as you pray for blessing upon your enemies?

For Contemplative Action

Throughout the day, look into people's eyes as you pass by them or while you are in conversation. Send every individual a loving thought. See if you can note the color of each person's eyes. Do you notice the beauty of the light of the individual's eyes, and the reflection of the image of God? Practices like this can bring us into the present moment where we connect with others on the level of our collective humanity.

---

[66] Thomas Merton, *New Seeds of Contemplation* (New York: New Directions, 1961), 177

8

Courage in the Public Square

> Courage in the public sphere means that one is to go against majority opinion ... in the name of the truth. ~ Vaclav Havel

> *They went to Capernaum; and when the Sabbath came, he entered the synagogue and taught. They were astounded at his teaching, for he taught them as one having authority, and not as the scribes. Just then there was in their synagogue a man with an unclean spirit, and he cried out, "What have you to do with us, Jesus of Nazareth? Have you come to destroy us? I know who you are, the Holy One of God." But Jesus rebuked him, saying, "Be silent, and come out of him!" And the unclean spirit, convulsing him and crying with a loud voice, came out of him. They were all amazed, and they kept on asking one another, "What is this? A new teaching—with authority! He commands even the unclean spirits, and they obey him." At once his fame began to spread throughout the surrounding region of Galilee. ~ Mark 1:21-28*

Established Western Christianity sustains an uneasy relationship with the idea of speaking prophetic truth to political leaders. As Christianity aligned itself with political power, religious leaders taught questioning the authority of the government betrayed God's will. The church denounced protest as an act of assertiveness that was incompatible with following Christ. Carefully constructed theology offered biblical justification for the power of government, and sometimes ratified its abuses. It was a win-win proposition.

Establishment theology allowed the Church to impose Christ on others with the backing of the government's might, and governments could increase their control with the Church's blessing. Christendom's theologians, quoting the Apostle Paul, taught that Christians must submit to the government as a way to surrender to God's will.

Victorian Americans relished images of Jesus as the Subdued Savior – a sympathetic and gentle friend and helper. He stands at the door of the heart and knocks, politely waiting for an invitation. Jesus, the Meek-and-Mild Messiah, always turns the other cheek and then sits us on his lap and asks for trusting obedience from his children. Consider the words of Rev. John Todd in 1851, who wrote, "There was never a being who, in words so few, so simple, so childlike, bowed, subdued, and controlled as many hearts as Jesus Christ."[67] The Subdued Savior is sympathetic and gentle, a friend and helper.

Does this theology best serve our faith communities? Does it put the Church in the position of being a political puppet, as opposed to the bearer of the rebellious message of the Reign of God? Christian Churches in America have gotten used to being number one. We have a term for this: Christendom. Christendom is another way of referring to Christian territory or Christian Empire; the areas of the world where Christianity prevail. In the year 313, the Roman Emperor Constantine signed a document called the Edict of Milan. Before the Edict of Milan, Christianity was an illegal religion in the Roman Empire. After the Edict of Milan, Christianity changed rapidly from a banned and often persecuted minority to the authorized religion of the Roman Empire. Christianity moved from the margins to the center of society and that movement re-engineered the church's DNA. Christendom developed ideas like: the creation of a Christian culture; the assumption that most were Christian by birth; the idea that political power was divinely authorized; and the definition of "orthodoxy" which was

---

67 Stephen J. Nichols, *Jesus Made in America: A Cultural History from the Puritans to The Passion of the Christ* (Downers Grove: IVP, 2008), 84

determined by powerful church leaders with state support. Christianity's presence in the halls of political power insured increased wealth for the church and called for the use of political and military force to impose Christian practices.

As Christianity aligned itself with political power, Christian leaders taught it was against God's will to question the authority of the government. However peaceable one's protest might be, however passive the demonstration, however humble the approach to those in authority, protest was wrong. No matter whether they are good or evil, political rulers were appointed by God and ought to be obeyed. This attitude still exists in some churches today. Some preach that resistance to government is rebellion against God and those who resist God must be punished. Some teach that Christians are called to live quiet, tranquil, peaceful lives with a submissive attitude toward those who lead us, acquiescing to rulers as we pray for their salvation. Writing in the *Christian Post* online, columnist Bethany Blankley states,

> The Christian worldview teaches that God removes rulers and puts them in power – both good and evil – for his purposes (Daniel 2:21; 4:17). All political leaders are appointed by God and nothing is beyond his control … If a Christian believes that God is in control, then he/she will submit to the ruling authorities and proclaim his/her faith by obeying God to be at peace with all men.[68]

Let's consider another perspective from the Christian New Testament. In the text quoted at the top of this chapter, a demon-possessed man confronts Jesus. The man is an unwilling participant in a social and religious system, which labels and excludes certain classes of people. Jesus chooses to heal this man, and in doing so provokes conflict. In Mark's gospel Jesus heals others as an act of public protest. Jesus protests a religious system that dominates and eliminates certain people. With all eyes on him, Jesus

---

68 Bethany Blankley, "The Oxymoron of Christian Protest," *The Christian Post* (April 23, 2012), http://www.christianpost.com/news/the-oxymoron-of-christian-protest-73704/.

engages in subversive public action, restoring the unhealthy man to wholeness. Throughout the Christian Gospels, whenever Jesus heals the sick, conflict escalates between Jesus and the authorities. When Jesus heals people, he challenges the power of the religious establishment. He symbolically resists the corrupted religious systems that segregate, stigmatize, and oppress people. Jesus calls his community to a fuller understanding of love, mercy, and justice.

Healing is an act of protest. And protest is a form of healing. Prayerful action moves us from despair to empowerment, from the restrictions of the self to a wider vision, and from the individual to the collective.

We live in revolutionary times. All over the globe, people are revolting against old systems of exploitation and oppression. New systems of justice and equality are being born. In our own country, we see a revolution of values. People are coming to an understanding that the purpose of government is not to gain capital through the wholesale disenfranchisement of people. Religion is growing in an understanding that its role is not to exclude, dominate or threaten those who go against systems of oppressive purity.

The fight for marriage equality in Maryland (and it was a fight!) serves as an example. In 2012, the congregation I serve took a very public stand in support of equal marriage rights for all consenting adult couples. The congregation considered marriage equality to be a civil right and a human right. Their faith led them to envision a local community, a state, and a country where no one is sanctioned or excluded for being gay. Spiritual activists in the congregation went door to door, coordinated phone banks, posted on social media, and visited state legislators to let voters know that not all churches opposed same-sex marriage. Members of the congregation wanted to let the world know there is such a thing as loving, thinking, faith-filled Christians who believe that religious institutions should include the LGBTQ+ community. Even though their stance put them at odds with more conservative religious traditions, and even some state legislators, they saw their public protest as an act of healing.

The Space Between 69

If we have learned anything from world events over the past years, it is that strong and loud public protest helps protect those who are most vulnerable. Consider these words from Czech playwright-turned-president Vaclav Havel:

> Courage in the public sphere means that one is to go against majority opinion (at the same time risking losing one's position) in the name of the truth. And I have always strongly admired historic personalities who have been capable of doing exactly this . . . Becoming a dissident is not something that happens overnight. You do not simply decide to become one. It is a long chain of steps and acts.[69]

Courage in the public sphere means going against majority opinion, over the long haul, in the name of the truth. This can be a terrifying prospect for some emerging protesters. There are at least three issues that hold religious people back from engaging the public square as spiritual activists.

Issue 1: We can be gullible. We often think too highly of people in power, believing elected officials represent their constituencies and not their own political ambitions. We assume our leaders are working for a more just world that supports the common good, sometimes naively. I realized my gullibility while attending a clergy prayer breakfast and lobby day for Marriage Equality in Annapolis. We took our message to three different state delegates who opposed the state's Civil Marriage Protection Act. Each one of them assuaged us with sweetness. They listened respectfully, but when it came time to commit, each dismissed us by saying, "Thanks for your time. I need to look more closely at the bill before I decide." I left Annapolis assuming they would truly consider supporting LGBTQ+ rights in our state, and I was disappointed not by opposition, but by the unwillingness to be honest with us and to vote in ways that might be unpopular with some of their constituents. I forgot that some in power do not always work for the common

---

69   Vaclav Havel, "Speak Truth to Power" (2010), http://blogs.nysut.org/sttp/defenders/vaclav-havel/.

good. Courage in the public sphere means confronting political laziness in the name of the truth.

Issue 2: We seek revenge. Scientist Michael McCullough explains that human beings have a hard-wired instinct, almost a craving, for revenge. If we experience fear of the unknown and some degree of insecurity and vulnerability in our souls, as long as we feel like we have to defend our honor, there is the likelihood of acting on our primal urge to hurt those who hurt us. But, as humorist Josh Billings once said, "There is no revenge so complete as forgiveness." McCullough thinks that *forgiveness* is also hard-wired in us. Humans tolerate deficits and excuse mistakes in others all the time, not just with those we love but people we work with. We forgive people hundreds of times a day without thinking much about it. As a species, it is in our best interest to forgive others. Our survival depends on being able to collaborate and work together.[70] What happens when you cannot work together, though? What do we do when the rift is too great, when the world seems wild and you no longer want to be complicit in the harmful decisions of those in whom you have put your trust?

Issue 3: Speaking truth to power is dangerous business. Speaking truth to power often enough can get us hurt. Exploring the intersections between politics and faith may get you fired. Speaking truth to power jeopardizes our perceptions of comfort and need and compels us to live simpler, less cluttered lives.

In the face of cowardice, gullibility, and fear, why in the world would we talk about speaking truth to power and the need for healing protest? Because some political, corporate, and religious leaders stand in servitude to the arrogance of power and its corrupting influences. Because we live in a time when some religious leaders take people down twisted paths that shame those who are different and exclude others. Because some political leaders bring us down irresponsible paths that offer Americans no hope of ever providing such basics as a sound education, adequate health care, and

---

70 Krista Tippett, *Einstein's God: Conversations about Science and the Human Spirit* (New York: Penguin Books, 2010), 171-195.

meaningful employment for all who live in our country. Because some public officials lead us down villainous paths that lead to war and destruction for personal gain instead of peace. Because some corporate interests lead us down miscreant paths that desecrate the beauty and integrity of the natural world and squander Earth's irreplaceable resources. Because some of us walk down folly-filled paths that disregard such simple lessons learned by every kindergartner, such as: we should tell the truth and share what we have, and do unto others as we want them to do unto us.

Spiritual activism involves grappling with the moral ambiguity of political life. Spiritual activists are willing to offer support for politicians when they make decisions that support the betterment and flourishing of all people. Spiritual activists also wonder, in a practical sense, whether our support even matters to politicians. What can the political support of the religious left be worth? As Rev. Michael-Ray Mathews, director of clergy organizing at PICO National Network reminds us, "It is important that politicians know that [clergy] are not just leaders in the community, not just members of faith communities, but that we are active voters. That we actually show up."[71]

Admittedly, political engagement is a morally vexing issue for some people. The entanglement of church and state creates a powerful ambivalence. So, spiritual activists ask whether the risk is worth the benefit. Contemplative action is not just a sentimental response to needs that we see around the world. Mathews reminds us political engagement is, "a reflection of how God created the world to be. It reflects a reality that existed before and ought to exist again. We're reflecting a truth, not a political program."[72] Policy objectives must flow from faith. But for people to have faith in the policy objectives, they must first have faith in the faithfulness of their leaders in governments, corporations, and other institutions. Compassion and inclusion are not only essential American values, but are also issues for spiritual activists to bring to light in an age of

---

71   Dionne, et. al., 31-32.
72   Dionne, et. al., 32.

growing inequality and extreme political polarization. At a time of deep mistrust of politics, Wall Street, and institutionalized religion, spiritual activists who engage with public life have both an opportunity and an obligation to challenge, to inspire, and to heal.[73]

In the Christian tradition, Communion/Eucharist is one of the most important, subversive, truth-speaking liturgies that we observe. It represents the end of false authority and the beginning of true authority that Jesus enacts at the beginning of his public ministry. It tells the story of the vanquishing of death and the renewal of life. It annuls human domination and offers foretaste of peace. Communion is a place where Christians can be honest about failure. It is a setting where participants are valued not by a paycheck or the color of one's skin, age, ability, gender identity or sexuality, but simply as people united in love. We gain strength to speak truth to power by participating in a love that can transform our lives and the world itself. As modern-day mystic John Philip Newell reminds us, part of what needs to be "re-membered" between us is the beauty of our oneness. We have each lived with dismemberment, a tearing apart of what belongs together. When we re-member, we can recover radical amazement which is the true basis for understanding.[74] In communion, we are called to re-member all the blessings we have received from God and all the ways in which, neighbors, stranger, even enemies – all of creation – take part in this blessing. We are called to re-member all the ties and duties that bind us to others.[75] We may celebrate the Lord's Table in different ways, but we share the same meal. At the Table, spiritual activists remember that all who profess faith, in all its assorted expressions, are truly a diverse body who form one loaf, giving thanks, praying, and working for the restored unity of humanity.

---

73 Dionne, et. al., 52.
74 John Philip Newell, *A New Harmony: The Spirit, the Earth, and the Human Soul* (San Francisco: Jossey-Bass, 2011), 50.
75 Robert A Rimbo, *Why Worship Matters* (Minneapolis: Augsburg ,2004), 59.

The Space Between

For Conversation

- Do you have a belief that people of faith should not in public protest? Where does that belief come from? Are those theologies still a good fit for you?
- What are the fears that hold you back from public protest as an expression of faith?
- When is fear an appropriate response to the call to courage in the public square? When might fear be an excuse for inaction?

For Active Contemplation: Prayer Walking

For those who are uncomfortable diving into public protest, start with small steps, literally, by going on individual and small group prayer walks around your neighborhood. Prayer walking is prayer in motion with awareness.

1. Before you begin, take three deep, healing breaths. Breathe in peace. Exhale joy. Invite the Spirit to join you. Remember you are walking to become aware of your world and how you fit into it.
2. Begin to walk slowly. What do you see, hear, smell, and feel? As you walk, offer thoughts and words of gratitude.
3. Continuing to walk in a spirit of prayer, you become aware of the needs around you. What do you notice that you have never perceived before? Maybe you see signs in your neighborhood that are troublesome. Or maybe your neighborhood is picture perfect by all appearances, but you happen to know firsthand some of the anguish that lies behind closed doors. What are you feeling as you walk? As you become aware of your feelings and responses, offer them as prayer.
4. As you walk, does a sacred verse, a line of a hymn, or a prayer refrain come to mind? If so, try breathing those words into the neighborhood as a response.
5. After completing several prayer walks, you will begin to become more aware of the space between the deep needs of the world and your desire to be a healing presence. This awareness

is the beginning of activism, and perhaps a chance to step into faith-based advocacy for the needs in your community.

For Contemplative Action: Celebrate a Non-Violent Communion

Many liturgists from various Christian traditions are experimenting with non-violent communion liturgies. In a world that celebrates violence, many wonder whether violence should also be represented in our most sacred liturgies. Consider what the condition of our faith communities might be like if the Great Thanksgiving said something like the following: "On the night before he went forth to his life-giving death, like a Lamb led to slaughter, rejecting violence, loving his enemies, and praying for his persecutors, Jesus bestowed upon his disciples the gift of a New Commandment:

> *"I give you a new commandment, that you love one another. Just as I have loved you, you also should love one another."*[76]

The sacrament becomes a creative opportunity to experience grace in action through a person who rejected violence, forgave everyone, prayed for persecutors, and returned good for evil.[77] Appendix E includes a sample non-violent liturgy for Communion, written in celebration for a service of interfaith awareness and based on the writings of feminist theologian Sr. Elizabeth Johnson.

---

76   John 13:34.
77   See *Emmanuel Charles McCarthy, The Nonviolent Eucharistic Jesus: A Pastoral Approach. Center for Christian Nonviolence*, http://www.centerforchristiannonviolence.org/data/Media/NV_Eucharist_PastoralApproach_01d.pdf.

9

Economic Life

What did you do once you knew? ~ Drew Dellinger

Our Gross National Product … counts air pollution and cigarette advertising … it counts special locks for our doors and the jails for people who break them. It counts the destruction of the redwood and the loss of our natural wonder in chaotic sprawl. It counts …nuclear warheads and armored cars for the police to fight the riot in our cities … and the television programs which glorify violence in order to sell toys to our children. Yet, the Gross National Product does not allow for the health of our children, the quality of their education or the joy of their play. It does not include the beauty of our poetry or the strength of our [relationships], the intelligence of our public debate or the integrity of our public officials. It measures neither our wit nor our courage, neither our wisdom nor our learning, neither our compassion nor our devotion to our country. It measures everything … except that which makes life worthwhile." ~ Robert Kennedy, speaking at the University of Kansas in 1968

America's middle class is in trouble. For the past 30 years, income stagnates while the costs of life's necessities continue to rise. Even for those with jobs, the promise of economic growth failed to deliver. Income for the typical middle-class household fell over the past 15 years. For years, Gallup has asked Americans about their biggest financial concern (Figure 1). Those in the middle class have consistently said they are most worried about not earning enough money, the high cost of living, and risks such as maintaining a decent standard of living in retirement and losing their job. Sadly,

Americans have also been telling pollsters, even before the start of the 2008 recession, they think their children will be worse off than they are.[78]

	18-49 years %	50-64 years %	65+ years %
Cost of owning/renting a home	16	10	4
Lack of money/Low wages	15	16	15
Unemployment/Loss of Job	13	9	5
Too much debt/Not enough money to pay debts	11	10	7
Healthcare costs	8	15	13
College expenses	8	5	2
High cost of living/Inflation	5	5	7
Lack of savings	4	3	2
Retirement savings	3	8	3
Energy costs/Oil and gas prices	3	2	2
Taxes	3	3	5
Transportation/Commuting costs	2	1	1
The stock market/Investments	2	5	7
Interest rates	1	2	1
Controlling spending	1	*	*
State of the Economy	1	3	3
Social Security	0	0	1
None	12	11	26
Other	1	3	2
No opinion	3	1	2

* Less than 0.5%
GALLUP POLL

FIGURE 1

78 Frank Newport, "Americans Have Widespread Personal Financial Concerns," *Gallup*, http://www.gallup.com/poll/117817/americans-widespread-personal-financial-concerns.aspx.

Instead of addressing the needs of the poor and America's shrinking middle class, American economic policy took our impressive gross domestic product and redistributed it to the rich. The share of domestic income going to the middle class has declined for decades. The poorest fifth of American households have seen their after-tax income increase by 18%. The richest fifth, have seen real income increases of 65%. For the top 1%, real income went up 275%. America is now a land of economic insecurity for most, and a playground of unprecedented wealth for a small minority. We live in an unequal society where those on top can enforce their will against people who have less. Those on the bottom have little reason to believe they will get a fair shake. No wonder we sense that our politics are permeated by distrust.

If the middle class is at risk, then the new American Economy also hosts a population of at-risk families. Tens of millions of people live in poverty, although many refuse to think of themselves as poor. Some make daily choices as to which necessities they will have to live without. Many work part- or full-time, but on that basis, are still unable to lift their families out of poverty. Others are physically or emotionally unable to work. Many lack the family, educational, and community support important for making good choices in their lives. Although those living in poverty are particularly visible in cities, their more hidden reality in suburban, small town, and rural areas can be just as painful. A greater proportion of non-white citizens live in conditions of poverty. There is nothing generous about our national definition of poverty. In 2017, the official U.S. poverty line for a family of four was an income of just below $24,600, or about $473 a week. That was the ceiling, not the average. More than 40% of poor U.S. families have incomes of less than half the poverty line. A fifth of American children live in poverty and two-fifths in low-income households – up 33% since 2000.[79]

---

79 David Madland, "Making Our Middle Class Stronger," *Center for American Progress* (August 1, 2012), http://www.americanprogress.org/

If the economic arena becomes a reigning power for Americans, then the question arises: in what or whom shall people of faith place our trust and hope? We cannot place our hope in the Gross Domestic Product. We cannot place our hope in unlimited economic growth. Neither Wall Street, nor K Street, nor Madison Avenue have our communities' best interests on their agenda. And even though we have heard it before, it bears repeating: Money does not buy happiness. You may have heard the joke, "Those who say money can't buy happiness just don't know where to shop!" Research shows money really does not buy happiness among the more affluent. Study after study show income is a weak generator of well-being. Do you know what produces happiness? The answer is complicated, but one reply is: "Other people." We flourish in settings with warm, nurturing, and rewarding interpersonal relationships. And we flourish best when we are giving, not getting.[80]

The Christian faith tradition records that Jesus spoke often about economics. We might summarize the message as follows: That which we keep to ourselves, that which we hoard, that which we take at the expense of other's survival, we keep from the common good. That which we give to the least of those among us, we give to the common good.

From the vantage point of faith, spiritual activists seek a different vision for the American economy: sufficient, sustainable

---

issues/economy/report/2012/08/01/12034/making-our-middle-class-stronger/.

Robert B Reich, "The Political Roots of Widening Inequality," *The American Prospect* 26:2 (Spring, 2015), 27-30.

Dorian T. Warren, "Putting Families First: Good Jobs for All," Center *for Community Change*, et. al. (2015).

"Poverty Guidelines," U.S. Health and Human Services, https://aspe.hhs.gov/poverty-guidelines.

80 Andrew Blackman, "Can Money Buy You Happiness?" *WSJ* (November 10, 2014), https://www.wsj.com/articles/can-money-buy-happiness-heres-what-science-has-to-say-1415569538.

livelihood for all. That language comes from a study put out in 1999 by the Evangelical Lutheran Church of America. Their statement affirms we are nurtured, sustained, and held accountable inter-dependent relationships.

- People of faith realize that what human beings want is not necessarily what they need for the sake of life.
- People of faith acknowledge that what is in our interest must be placed in the context of what is good for our "neighbor."
- People of faith recognize that intense competitiveness can destroy relationships and work against the reconciliation and cooperation God desires among people.
- People of faith affirm that God promises a world where there is enough for everyone, if only we would learn how to use and share what God gives for the sake of all.
- People of faith insist that economic growth must be evaluated by its short-term, and long-term effects on the well-being of all creation and people, especially those who are poor.[81]

Considering these realities, spiritual activists serve the transcendent needs of the common good by serving the least of those among us. We provide counsel, food, clothing, shelter, and money for people in need, in ways that respect human dignity. We develop mutual, face-to-face, relationships between people who have enough and people living in poverty. We advocate for public and private policies that effectively address the causes of poverty. We support organizations and community-based efforts that enable low-income people to obtain sufficient, sustainable livelihoods. And we continue working to eradicate racism and sexism in economic life. Most of all, spiritual activists seek to expand human vision and transform community priorities. We become restless when we see less than what we think God intends for the world. Spiritual activists act, pray, and hope that through economic life

---

81 "A Social Statement on Sufficient, Sustainable Livelihood for All by the ELCA," *Evangelical Lutheran Church in America* (1999), https://www.elca.org/en/Faith/Faith-and-Society/Social-Statements/Economic-Life.

there truly will be sufficient, sustainable livelihood for all. Drew Dellinger's poem, "hieroglyphic staircase," serves as a manifesto for spiritual activism and economic life.

> *it's 3:23 in the morning*
> *and I'm awake*
> *because my great great grandchildren*
> *won't let me sleep*
> *my great great grandchildren*
> *ask me in dreams*
> *what did you do while the planet was plundered?*
> *what did you do when the earth was unraveling?*
>
> *surely you did something*
> *when the seasons started failing?*
>
> *as the mammals, reptiles, birds were all dying?*
>
> *did you fill the streets with protest*
> *when democracy was stolen?*
>
> *what did you do*
> *once*
> *you*
> *knew?*[82]

Spiritual activists ask questions and look for answers through contemplative action and active contemplation:
- What if God is asking of us?
- What did we do when our economic household was being plundered?
- What did we do when our democracy unraveled?
- Did we fill the streets when equality was stolen?
- What will we tell our great, great grandchildren?
- What did we do once we knew?

---

82 Drew Dellinger, "Hieroglyphic Staircase" (September 29, 2009), http://drewdellinger.org/pages/video/187/hieroglyphic-stairway.

The answers foresee an America where the pursuit of happiness is not about more spending, but in the growth of human solidarity, solid democracy, and devotion to the public good; an America where the benefits of economic activity are widely and equitably shared; an America where the environment is sustained for current and future generations; an America where the virtues of simple living, community self-reliance, and respect for nature prevail; and an America where no citizens or immigrants are left to fend for themselves alone and afraid. [83]

In this new way of life together, we refuse to keep holding on to what we already have while grabbing even more as if our life depends on it. We do not keep gathering and hoarding so we must build ever-bigger garages or rent ever-larger storage units. Faith gives us a vision of a new life together, including the vision of an economy in which we hold on only to give, and we gather only to share.

What will we do, now that we know?

For Conversation

Consider your personal beliefs and theology around the word *labor*. What are some of the ways we determine the fair rewards for labor? What stories from scripture or your religious history back up those claims? Who or what guarantees that you are fairly compensated for your work? What groups of people do not have any guarantees they will be fairly compensated for their work? Ask the same questions with different words like: fairness, growth, equity, generosity, sustainability, or abundance.

For Active Contemplation: Spiritual Reflection on Economics

As a spiritual practice, write a reflection on your understanding of faith and economics from three different theological poles

---

[83] James Gustave Speth, *America the Possible: Manifesto for a New Economy* (New Haven: Yale University Press, 2012).

or angles: History & Tradition, Cultural Resources, and Personal Experience. As you reflect on the interaction of these poles, here are some questions and suggestions to guide your thinking:

- **History and Tradition:** What is your theology of economic life? What sources inform your theology (e.g. scripture, creeds, historical writings, theological traditions, religious teachings and/or media)?
- **Cultural Resources:** How do racial/ethnic background, socioeconomic and educational levels, gender, cultural practices and norms, geography, and multi-generational expectations influence how you view economic life? In what ways are your views shaped by dominant culture or multi-cultural contexts? In what ways did your extended family system shape your experience with money?
- **Personal Experience:** Identify times and places where you have a prevailing response or a patterned reaction to money in your personal history. Where and how might those reactions have been learned? Do you notice that you have a particular response across the board, or do you have different responses for different roles you play in life? Describe how those roles vary. Are you satisfied with your responses to economic life? If so, how so? If not, why not?

For Contemplative Action

Does your denomination or religious tradition have a public statement on economic justice? Most mainline Christian denominations and some Evangelical Christian groups have statements and study guides. Take some time to read and study your tradition's public theology on economics. Here are a few:

- **Evangelical Lutheran Church of America:** "Sufficient, Sustainable Livelihood for All." (http://www.elca.org/Faith/Faith-and-Society/Social-Statements/Economic-Life).

- **United Methodist Church:** "Pathways to Economic Justice" (http://www.umc.org/what-we-believe/pathways-to-economic-justice).
- **Presbyterian Church (USA)/Reformed:** The Accra Confession: Covenant for Justice in the Economy and the Earth (http://wcrc.ch/accra/the-accra-confession).
- **United Church of Christ Economic Justice Resolutions** (http://www.ucc.org/justice_economic-justice_resolutions#general).
- **Episcopal General Convention** (http://archive.episcopalchurch.org/109303_104875_ENG_HTM.htm).
- **United States Conference of Catholic Bishops:** Economic Justice for All (http://www.usccb.org/upload/economic_justice_for_all.pdf).
- **Evangelical:** The Oxford Declaration on Christian Faith and Economics (https://www.calvin.edu/~pribeiro/DCM-Lewis-2009/Lewis/Economics-1.doc).
- **Anabaptist:** Anabaptist/Mennonite Faith and Economics by Calvin Wall Redekop, Victor A. Krahn, Samuel J. Steiner. Lanham: University Press, 1994).
- **American Baptist:** Resolution on Economic Justice (http://www.abc-usa.org/wp-content/uploads/2012/06/ECONOMIC-JUSTICE.pdf).

10

Pity, Compassion, and Power

> Hillel said: The more flesh, the more worms; the more possessions, the more worry; the more servants, the more thievery. The more Torah, the more life; the more study, the more wisdom; the more charity, the more peace. ~ Pirke Avot 2:8

> *Then Jesus went about all the cities and villages, teaching in their synagogues, and proclaiming the good news of the kingdom, and curing every disease and every sickness. When he saw the crowds, he had compassion for them, because they were harassed and helpless, like sheep without a shepherd.* ~ Matthew 9:35-36

Take a moment to become aware of yourself. Become aware of your own body and how you feel at this moment, aware of the sounds of people who may be around you right now. Pay attention to particular smells and sounds. As you read the following descriptions of different people and situations, pay attention to where in your body you may feel a reaction. After each description, you are invited to repeat a phrase in the quietness of your own mind. Are you ready?

Think about Syria. Some say Damascus is a place where it is easy to lose empathy for the suffering of others. Westerners tend to view conflicts in areas like Syria at the macro level. It is easy to overlook what small groups are doing to survive. Though the Syrian conflict is a convoluted mess of revolutionaries and an intractable dictatorial regime, it is also much more than that. The civil war conflict created over two million children displaced by fighting, spread out over several camps and orphanages across the region. These children have names and personal narratives, and they will inherit the future of Syria – or whatever is left of it.[84] I invite you to say to yourself, "I know sadness and fear. The children of Syria also know deep sadness and fear."

Imagine another situation — a 15-year-old girl named Maria. She lives in Honduras where she works 12-hour days without any overtime pay. She is paid 50 cents an hour to make jeans, unprotected from exposure to dangerous chemicals. Maria works in difficult conditions with a long journey, interminable hours, and low wages. With no social safety net or benefits provided under Honduran labor laws, she is also exposed to violence, including sexual abuse. Say to yourself, "Just like me, Maria is trying to avoid suffering in her life."

Think about a politician with whom you have very different views. Say, "Just like me, he or she is human and learning about life."

Recall a friend, family member or a colleague with whom you find yourself in conflict. It could be a recent misunderstanding or a past argument. With that person in mind say, "Just like me, she or he is seeking joy, happiness and meaning in life."

For whom is it easier to feel compassion, those farther away from us or those closest to home? Even within our own faith communities, so many people suffer. It can feel as though there is not enough room in the world to embrace all the pain we experience. Each of us holds the suffering of the world in our body, just as some religious traditions teach that God holds the suffering of the world in a body. Christians call this idea *incarnation*.

I remember when I began to learn about the difference between embracing pain as an experience of pity versus the experience

---

84 "Voices from Syria," P*eace and Conflict Monitor* (October 10, 2014), http://www.monitor.upeace.org/innerpg.cfm?id_article=1067. See also "Syrian Children Under Siege," UNICEF, https://www.unicefusa.org/mission/emergencies/child-refugees/syria-crisis.

of compassionate power sharing. I was a freshly-ordained pastor serving a small rural church for about a year when I met Janet, a 17-year old mom with a baby girl. At age 17, Janet was romanced by a 30-year-old man who got her pregnant. They lived together, trying to raise their new daughter. Rumors around town alleged the boyfriend abused her. One afternoon, when I came home from work, Janet sat at our kitchen table with my wife. Janet decided to leave her boyfriend who, according to her, was verbally and emotionally brutal. She felt like a prisoner in her own house and she wanted out. Since she was still 17 and a minor, her decision posed some challenges. Janet quickly learned how to navigate "the system": food assistance, welfare, and family court. When she was not living with a family member, she and her baby stayed at a meager motel room, funded by Social Services. We gave her grocery money to help her get by. My wife watched her baby free of charge. The church deacons bought Christmas gifts for Janet and her baby. Family court eventually awarded her full custody.

After a few months, Janet moved back in with her boyfriend. She would have rather lived with the abuse than have tolerated poverty. She still expected further financial charity and free babysitting. When rumors in our small town said she had moved back home with her boyfriend I felt so naive, as if our assistance went for nothing. Was Janet ever given the tools to be a better-functioning person, a more skilled mother, or a healthier member of our community? Did we do the right thing? Did we offer pity? Did we share power?

I also learned about pity and compassion from Luke. One Sunday morning, just before the beginning of worship, a mom pulled me aside and told me that her stepson Luke tried to kill himself by jumping off a three-story building. Two weeks later, I visited Luke at a hospital after the last of his extensive reconstructive surgeries. Luke was a 22-year-old young man whose eyes told the whole story: he was broken, his body crushed, and his emotions tormented by depression and loneliness. As it turned out, Luke had not tried to kill himself. While running away from a drug-deal-gone-bad, he attempted to leap off the roof to get away. In these situations, there is really nothing to say. It did not seem like the right time to lecture Luke on the consequences of bad decisions. There was no need to manipulate him with guilt. I wanted him to experience a sense of belonging, total love and full acceptance. What do we do when we are moved with compassion, but we do not know how to show it? What happens when we get just one chance to say the right thing, and we end up sitting silently, listening with understanding, and trying to be a friend? Could Luke have been encouraged to change his life, be a whole person, and become a healthier member of the community?

Jesus, love incarnate, divinity enfleshed, embraced the needs of the world in his body and said, "Here I am. I am present, I am fully here. How can I use my life and gifts to share my power?" He had a way of seeing potential in people like street women, tax collectors, lepers, and those marginalized by society. Jesus saw value in each of them. There is an important phrase from the passage quoted at the beginning of this chapter. Jesus, "had compassion on them." With embodied compassion, Jesus healed. He shared power. He offered life with new possibilities. Unrestrained, unconditional compassion is the call of every spiritual activist, even if it means being taken advantage of or giving some of that which we value.

I learned something important in my relationships with Janet and Luke in those early years of my ministry. I wanted to offer compassion, but I ignored my own inner journey. I had not worked out why I needed to help. I lacked honesty about my own needs and motives before I offered to fix someone else's mess. The compassion I offered was more like pity. Whether it helps the other or not, offering pity makes the giver feel better, but pity only addresses symptoms, not causes.

Another word we can use to describe embodied compassion is *mitzvah*. *Mitzvah* is a Hebrew word, usually defined as a commandment, a good deed, or religious act. A *mitzvah* is an act of goodness or a religious observance. However, *mitzvah* is much more than that. It can also mean human capacity.⁸⁵ It is a crucial principal in the journey of the spiritual activist. While we hold the needs of the world in our bodies, instead of offering pity or charity, we offer a *mitzvah*. We say, "I am present, I am fully here, how can I use my life and gifts to help you claim your power?" Compassion is much more profound when we offer a *mitzvah* out of deep inner awareness.

Compassion like this can take on many faces. Compassion can be soft and nurturing, and at the same time it can be tough love. Compassion can be receptive and listening, or it can be active and practical, or anywhere along that spectrum. Compassion can be deeply patient, or recklessly impatient. Compassion can be sitting with someone, or taking someone's hand to lead the way. Compassion can be neat and clear. Compassion can be messy and clumsy. No matter what, compassion is about presence. Where do you find yourself skillful in helping others claim their power? Where are your growing edges?

Transformation comes when we share what we have with others who are in need. Transformation comes when we know who we are: wounded people who know sadness and fear; fearful people who want to avoid suffering and find happiness; growing people who are learning about life and trying to find joy and meaning. We do not have to worry about compassion. It exists in abundance. We wake up to it and reach out for it. We share it. We live it. We hold compassion in our bodies. When we learn the power of *mitzvah*, we take part in the transformation of the world through service, justice and compassion; when we know who we are – one of the Earth's beloved, just like all other residents of this planet.⁸⁶

---

85   Byron L. Sherwin, *Faith Finding Meaning: A Theology of Judaism* (Oxford: Oxford University Press, 2009), 120. See also, Bender Braha, "Experiential Torah," *Arachim*, http://arachimusa.org/ArticleDetail.asp?ArticleID=1635.
86   "Pirke Avot 2:8," *Ancient Wisdom for Us Today*, http://ancientwisdom4ustoday.org/?page_id=844.

For Conversation

While we use the word "justice" in our religious traditions, we are not always clear on what we mean. Sometimes "justice" is defined in terms of *equality*: everyone should get or have the same amount, regardless of how hard they work. Other traditions define "justice" in terms of *equity*: people should get benefits in proportion to what they contributed to producing those benefits. Some believe in equity with a bottom "safety-net" which protects people who, because of misfortune or disability, are unable to work or even help themselves. Others believe justice requires that some people should receive a higher share of goods and services from a common purse, which are redistributed according to one's need and ability to work. How do you define justice? How is your definition reinforced by, or stand in contrast to, your religious tradition? Does your definition of justice include room for compassion, empathy, and power sharing?

For Active Contemplation: Pity Party

One way to notice the difference between pity and power sharing in your dealings with others is to first recognize when you are seeking pity for yourself. We all have times when we want another to feel sorry for us and we want another to solve our problems. You may be seeking pity if you:

- Regularly tell others that life or parts of your life are unfair,
- Repeatedly talk about how someone harmed you,
- Draw attention to your problems and ask why they always happen to you,
- Secretly wish for negative outcomes so you can talk about them,
- Get caught up in your own head and become unaware of other people,
- Look at another's misfortune through how it negatively impacts you.

How might these pity-seeking behaviors be transformed by a regular practice of active contemplation?

For Contemplative Action: Empowerment Audit

Power sharing is the process of opening opportunities for individuals or groups to enhance and enrich their lives. Groups with less power in society, or experiencing political injustice, seek empowerment as a road to equality or betterment of their position. Empowerment audits examine the factual basis of both sides' arguments and seek to bring about a mutually satisfactory resolution. Conduct an Empowerment Audit of your faith community. Here are some questions to start with:

- What do we mean when we say we want to share power with people?
- What are the characteristics of an empowered person?
- What organizational characteristics facilitate compassionate power sharing?
- Do we really want self-empowered people? How do we know?
- What can spiritual activists do to facilitate compassionate power sharing?
- Does our faith community's structure and governance promote or hinder power sharing?
- In what ways does our faith community give people meaning in their work together? Do we care about what we are doing?
- Do people in our faith community feel listened to? How can we find out?
- Do members of our faith community feel that we are making a positive impact as a community? How can we find out?
- How does our faith community feel about rewarding risk-taking and initiative?
- Whose voices were not included in our audit? Are they important to us? How can we invite their participation?

After you explore these questions, pick two or three areas of growth to work on. Develop some mutual goals and strategies to develop mutual, compassionate power sharing.

11

Isolation, Prayer, and Community Wisdom

What are our wounds? ~ Henri Nouwen

Prayer expresses who we are as humans in inter-connected relationship with one another and with the Spirit. Prayer is a path to peace. However, that path is not always easy. You may be familiar with the serenity prayer, or at least the beginning of it. It goes like this:

God grant me the serenity
to accept the things I cannot change;
courage to change the things I can;
and wisdom to know the difference.

The second part of the prayer – perhaps the less familiar part – goes something like this:

Living one day at a time;
Enjoying one moment at a time;
Accepting hardships as the pathway to peace;
Taking, as God did, this sinful world
as it is, not as I would have it;
Trusting that God will make all things right
if I surrender to God's Will;
That I may be reasonably happy in this life
and supremely happy with God
forever in the next.

Look back at the line that says, "accepting hardship as the pathway to peace." Sometimes we tell ourselves if we can solve all our problems, eliminate all hardships, and remove all the causes of stress in our life, then we can find peace. We tend to believe the reasons for our anxieties lie in circumstances over which we have little or no control. If we can gain the upper hand over our problems, we will have serenity. Sometimes, we think we must fix life's problems on our own because God fell asleep on the job. We must draw upon our human capacities. No supernatural help is coming. That is why we struggle so hard to gain control over difficult people and impossible situations. We secretly tell ourselves that we will only be happy once we become more omnipotent. We try desperately to manipulate people and situations over which we have no control. We end up failing and we get upset because we always fall short in one way or another. What we eventually discover is the more we struggle against unmanageable circumstances, the further we are from the peace we seek. Can spiritual activists trust that hardship can be an opportunity and not the curse we may take it to be? Can we accept difficulty with grace, as if it were a gift we would have chosen for ourselves?

THEOSIS: UNITED IN LOVE

Eastern Christian sages taught a path to peace through a prayerful remembrance of a divine resource living deep within us. The Eastern Church calls it *theosis*. The idea of *theosis* is that, through daily contemplation, we become like God, slowly and steadily. With patience and practice, we arrive at union with the divine. God's aim for the world is for each of us to be restored to the full potential of our humanity, and our full potential is a lot bigger than we can imagine. We have the potential to be one with God and with all of creation. If we can reach full union with God, we will be able exist within God's love. As Eastern Orthodox Saint, Basil the Great, said, "The human vocation is to fulfill one's humanity by becoming God through grace."[87] United in love, we become divine. That is *theosis*. We cannot help but to become love in the flesh. And once we do that, we can hold one another in love. Tenderly. Gently. Prayerfully.

Spiritual activists look at hardship as a pathway to a much deeper and more enduring kind of peace; not dependent upon circumstances beyond our control, but upon loving union with the Transcendent. Poet Jane Hirshfield wrote a poem that speaks to the spiritual activist's need to engage in active contemplation when facing hardship.

> *There are names for what binds us:*
> *strong forces, weak forces.*
> *Look around you, you can see them:*
> *the skin that forms in a half-empty cup,*
> *nails rusting into the places they join,*
> *joints dovetailed on their own weight.*
> *The way things stay so solidly*
> *wherever they've been set down—*
> *and gravity, scientists say, is weak.*
>
> *And see how the flesh grows back*
> *across a wound, with a great vehemence,*
> *more strong*
> *than the simple, untested surface before.*
> *There's a name for it on horses,*
> *when it comes back darker and raised: proud flesh,*
>
> *as all flesh,*
> *is proud of its wounds, wears them*
> *as honors given out after battle.*[88]

---

87 Michael K. Marsh, "Theosis, the Human Vocation, " *Interrupting the Silence* (July 9, 2011), https://interruptingthesilence.com/2011/07/09/theosis-the-human-vocation/.

88 Jane Hirschfield, "For What Binds Us," *Poetry Foundation*, http://www.poetryfoundation.org/poem/186177.

Proud flesh is also known as granulation tissue. Treating proud flesh is an important and necessary part of healing a wounded horse. Horses are majestic animals but also fragile and thin-skinned. The most frustrating injury a horse can get is a cut on its lower leg where there is very little muscle or fat between skin and bone. The skin pulls apart, and it is virtually impossible to suture. The healing process can be deceptive. Healing appears rapid, but the new tissue keeps forming into pink, ugly lumps above the surrounding healthy tissue. That scar tissue is called proud flesh. It is a long, painful process to treat a horse with a wound on its lower leg. It requires patience and hope, courage and stamina. The horse hurts and does not want people messing with its wound. The horse sees the healer as the source of its pain and will most certainly kick. The wound hurts, the hardship is real, but with care and attention, with attentive love, that horse can heal up and run with stallions.[89]

Maybe people are not so different. We can become worn, weary, wounded, and wondering if these moments of life are gifts or curses. Then, in a flash of grace, in loving union, with patient attention, we can experience *theosis*. We can make peace with hardship by becoming the presence of healing love. We are changed. We are love. We rise.

SHARING WOUNDS IN COMMUNITY

Ministry can be wounding and isolating. One recent study indicates that while most ministers consider it a privilege to be a pastor, more than half of the survey respondents (55 percent) also agree with the statement, "I find that it is easy to get discouraged," and 55 percent say being in pastoral ministry makes them feel lonely at times.[90] A number of years ago, during a particularly difficult time in my ministry, I attended the annual conference of the

---

[89] Jayne Wilson, "Treating Proud Flesh: Excessive Granulation Tissue in Horses," *MyHorse.com*, http://myhorse.com/blogs/horse-care/illness-and-injuries/proud-flesh-in-horses/.

[90] "Poll: Many Pastors Feel Lonely, Discouraged," *Pastors.com* (October 24, 2011), http://pastors.com/poll-many-pastors-feel-lonely-discouraged/.

Academy of Parish Clergy; a gathering of ministers from across the country who foster excellence in the practice of ministry. At one casual gathering, some members of the Academy asked me about my story. I began to share my frustrations in ministry, the pains from serving in my congregation, and the friction with church staff members. When I finished, one of the long-timers in the group started laughing. Turning to his friend, he said, "Hey Bob, you had one of those churches, too! Remember?"

Bob laughed along, "I sure do! Remember the church secretary from hell?" Like war buddies showing off their scars, seasoned faith leaders began exposing their ministry-gone-bad stories. To this day, it remains one of the most comforting and healing experiences of my ministry. Hearing their stories, I no longer felt alone. I hoped that I would not only survive, but perhaps I would also be able to forgive myself and others. And maybe someday I might be able to laugh about it, too.

Looking back, part of my sense of abandonment was not just that I felt forsaken. I also nourished the I-can-do-it-myself-ishness that fed my forsakenness. I pictured myself as a lone minister made of coarseness and strength combined with acuteness and grit; a pastor with a practical inventive mind, restless passion, nervous energy, and principled individualism. I was a loner leader.

Spiritual activism can be a lonesome calling. Isolation comes easily. We can be tempted to think we are doing God's work alone, while others watch without commitment. Sometimes it feels as if nobody else cares as much as you do. You can feel persecuted and forsaken. Isolation can also lead to a false sense of responsibility. Since nobody else will help solve the problems of the world, you must shoulder the burden alone.

Spiritual activists cannot afford to do this work alone. We need groups of like-minded, committed peers who can assist us in maintaining our passion and perspective. One term for these groups is "communities of practice." The idea is based on the research and writing of Beverly Wenger and Etienne Traynor. A community of practice is a peer-learning group; people who share a concern or a passion for something they do and learn how to do it better as they interact regularly. In pursuing their interests, members of a community of practice engage in mutual activities and Conversations, help each other, and share information. They build relationships that encourage them to learn from each other. They develop a shared repertoire of resources: experiences, stories, tools, and ways of addressing recurring problems. This requires time and sustained interaction.

A community of practice is more than an *ad hoc* clergy group where members, who may come and go, eat a sandwich and brag about their work. Austin Seminary conducted a study of clergy communities of practice[91] and found that the most effective groups had:

- regular attendance and commitment,
- some sort of curriculum,
- a facilitator, and
- opportunities to connect in between meetings, via email, Facebook, etc.,

Austin Seminary stated that pastoral leaders who report rejuvenated ministries stay in their community of practice for three important reasons:

- the group provides accountability,
- the group experience is a source of interest in and the means for improving their ministry, and
- the group's leader or facilitator impressed them.

To ensure that a community of practice is most beneficial, the report suggests the following expectations:

- The group meetings should be regularly attended.
- The group process should be guided by a formal covenant.

---

91 "Is the Treatment the Cure? A Study of the Effects of Participation in Pastoral Leader Peer Groups," Austin Presbyterian Seminary (April, 2010), https://www.samford.edu/uploadedFiles/RCPE/Content/Is%20 the%20Treatment%20the%20Cure.pdf.

- The group should have a high-quality leader or facilitator.
- The group should be diverse.
- The group should provide intimacy and accountability.
- The group's practices should include expressing spirituality in creative ways, e.g. through art, music, literature or drama.

TEMENOS: SACRED SPACE

Spiritual activism requires spiritual depth, personal integrity, and effective leadership. Peer-learning groups are essential to this ongoing process of growth. We often wonder, "Where is God in our spiritual practice and what does God require of us?" Communities of practice become *temenos*, an ancient word for "sacred space" or the domain of the holy. *Temenos* refers to a universal instinct to create a protected, safe space in which to heal, reorganize, and regenerate the fragmented personality. Spiritual leaders who participate in communities of practice report that they not only feel safe to share what they cannot share elsewhere, but they also enter holy ground where they feel the presence of the divine. Peer groups invite growth through contemplative listening, accountability, and acceptance of diversity. Mutuality and reciprocity thrive in a place where silence is invited to be part of the language of the soul. Groups create sacred space when they create non-judgmental, welcoming, peace-filled processes in which trust, intimacy, sadness, and laughter can be shared.[92]

For spiritual activists, one purpose of a community of practice is to nurture one another on the journey toward forming a responsible society. In 1948, The General Assembly of the World Council of Churches developed the idea of "responsible society" as the goal of Christian action. The assembly wrote:

> For a society to be responsible under modern conditions, it is required that the people have freedom to control, to criticize, and to change their governments, that power be made

---

92 Penny Long Marler, et. al., *So Much Better: How Thousands of Pastors Help Each Other Thrive* (St. Louis: Chalice Press, 2013), 142.

responsible by law and tradition, and be distributed as widely as possible through the whole. For a society to be responsible under modern conditions, it is required that the people have freedom to control, to criticize, and to change their governments, that power be made responsible community.[93]

A responsible society fosters justice, participation, and the integrity of creation. Peer learning communities, as sacred ground, become places where groups practice justice in the ways they share leadership, resources, and common life. Groups may direct their learning toward the issues of spiritual activism on local, national, and international levels. In doing so, participants may come to understand God. Process theologian Marjorie Suchoki puts it like this:

> In God, the many are one everlastingly, each contributing to the others and receiving from others in the unity of God … It is not enough to confine oneself to one's own task: one must contribute to others and receive from others throughout the breadth of the work.[94]

Communities of practice as *temenos* can provide a hallowed ground where people are valued, equality is cherished, and everyone is respected. It is in this safe, sacred place where we know the presence of the Spirit who inspires with energy, intelligence, creativity, and love.

The moral: Spiritual activists need connection and community. It may be one of the most important things we do to remain focused on the work of making the world a more human and humane place.

For Conversation

- Think of a time when you felt wounded, isolated or burned out in your ministry. Describe your experience. What, if anything, helped you through the suffering?

---

93 Marler, 175
94 Marler, 177.

- When and where have you experienced *theosis*? How would you describe it using all your senses (what did it look like, smell like, feel like, sound like)?
- When and where have you experienced *temenos*? How would you describe it using all your senses (what did it look like, smell like, feel like, sound like)?
- When have you experienced a just, reciprocal, mutual community? How did it come into being? How was it sustained? What where the blessings? What were the challenges?

For Active Contemplation

A community of practice requires trust – the ability to depend on one another in fair, honest, and informal ways. Think about teams and communities in which you have participated.

- Describe the group and its function. Who was involved? How were people chosen to participate? Could you establish an environment of trust? What were the results?
- What can be replicated in other teams and communities?
- What would you avoid next time?
- In what ways did you (or not) experience *temenos*?

For Contemplative Action

This exercise is based on "Sustaining Self-Care: a tool for personal awareness" by Training for Change.[95] Participants get into groups of three and briefly introduce themselves to each other if they do not know each other. Then, they settle into a moment of silence to reflect on three questions: How do I come to the work of spiritual activism? What helps me sustain my work? What gets in the way of sustaining my work? Participants have 5-7 minutes each to share their stories.

When small groups are finished sharing, come back together as a large group. As each group reports back, invite participants to look for common themes. What motivates people? What gets in the way of sustainability? Make two lists: What Sustains You / What Depletes You. Do you notice any patterns? Help the group pay attention to forms of sustenance people already do that individuals can carry with them into their ministries.

Much of spiritual activism is about balance. There may be some wisdom in looking at the two lists together and how they relate to one's personal balance. Send people back into their original groups of three with the question: "What are the connections between what sustains you and what depletes you?" After several minutes, reflect again with the group-at-large.

---

95 "Sustaining Self-Care: a tool for personal awareness," *Training for Change*, https://www.trainingforchange.org/tools/sustaining-self-care-tool-personal-awareness.

12

Open Faith Communities

> Boundaries occupy the space
> between unity and purity.
> ~ Miroslav Volf, *Exclusion & Embrace*

Think about your faith community as a set — a collection of distinct objects, which, when grouped together, become an object of its own. Consider the numbers 2,4,6. They are individual numbers, but we can combine them into a set of even numbers {2,4,6...}. Sets are groups of objects with common characteristics: prime numbers, unicorns, tofu recipes, whatever ... we can make a set of it. Set Theory is a way of talking about what sets do and how they relate to each other.

We can talk about organizations as sets. When we look at organizations, we can see that they form around common social characteristics. Some organizations are called "bounded sets" (Figure 2). Bounded-set organizations have firm outer boundaries that must be crossed by those who want to belong to the organization. Bounded-set organizations have strict rituals, rules, and language that make it possible for others to know who is in and who is out. We could say that bounded set organizations tend to form a singular criterion that allows people to become members. Religious organizations are pros at this. Churches, for instance, tend to have coded religious language that newcomers do not always understand. Congregations have rituals and rules during worship, like when we sit and when we stand. The rules can be confusing to someone who wants to be part of the community but does not understand the characteristics of the congregation that make it come together as a set.

Some bounded-set religious organizations make "belonging" the requirement to become a member: "You must be one of us to be accepted." Others make "believing" a qualification for admittance: "If you believe in Jesus Christ as your Lord and Savior (or affirm the Apostle's Creed, or agree to our statement of faith), then you can be one of us." Still others require a certain type of "behavior": "Here is the list of moral and ethical requirements we hold as a congregation. No drinking, No swearing, No dancing. Follow the 10 commandments. If you obey our behavioral norm, you will be pure and can be part of our group."[96]

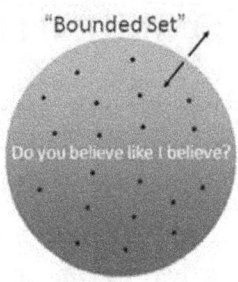

FIGURE 2

The model of "belonging as believing" is not necessarily a perilous theology. Some people need to belong, before they believe. Thinking about the interplay between belonging and believing can provide spiritual activists with an opportunity to think about how we nurture our core values and community life, rather than maintaining strict entrance requirements. An implicit theology of belonging can enhance a community's practice of welcome and hospitality. We can embody our core values in attractive, clear and deeply owned ways.[97]

However, we must also raise the question: Who gets to belong? Searching for an answer, some groups include everyone, obliterating boundaries and over-focusing on unity. Others focus on organizational purity and will not admit those who may pollute the faithful.

---

96 Jack Niewold, "Set Theory in Leadership," *Journal of Biblical Perspectives in Leadership* 2, no. 1 (Winter 2008), 46-47. See also, Andrew Marin, "Belong, Believe, Become," *Love Is an Orientation,* http://www.patheos.com/blogs/loveisanorientation/2011/02/belong-believe-become/#ixzz3RA6w9IDt.

97 Stuart Murray, *Post Christendom: Church and Mission in a Strange New World* (Milton Keynes: Paternoster, 2004), 310.

The Space Between

Ultimately, these are questions about how we navigate boundaries. Christian theologian Miroslav Volf writes that boundaries occupy the space between unity and purity. One side of the boundary is embrace — the will to give ourselves to others, to welcome them, to readjust our identities, and to make space for the other. On the other side of the boundary is the struggle against deception, injustice and violence.[98] A consistent pursuit of unity places one before the impossible choice between a chaos without boundaries and oppression with them. Enforcing purity in others is a form of exclusion. It stems from a belief that the source of evil lies outside of a person without considering that evil also lives inside a person. In extreme cases, those who are different will be excluded by elimination. Oppressors also exclude through assimilation, domination and abandonment.[99]

Spiritual Activists navigate the extremes of purity and unity, exclusion and embrace, by thinking about the ethical implications of theology and balancing the need for *belonging* and *believing* with reflections on *behavior*. We can think about behavior as a life-giving and generative quality of progressive movements. Belonging, believing, and behaving are central components of a community enactment of faith – they are all responses to grace. As we embrace our mutual values, communities can welcome others, just as those who practice faith feel welcomed by God. We can live faithfully and accountably. We find an identity rooted in a sense of belonging to the spirit of love, and energized by the community's life-giving behavior as it enacts its values. In so doing, we can dream about a brilliant future together.

There is another type of set in organizations that illustrate the idea of grace-filled communities. They are called *centered sets* (Figure 3). Where a bounded-set organization recognizes people in relationship to its boundary, a centered-set organization recognizes people in relationship to the center. If the bounded-set organization is like a traditional ranch with high fences to keep the right cattle

---

98   Volf, 29.
99   Volf, 64, 79.

in, the centered set organization is like an Outback ranch with a wellspring at its center. The Outback ranch has no fences, just a watering hole. The rancher does not need to control the livestock. The animals always come back to the center for water. The primary concern of those in this set is to bring others into relationship with the center.[100] Because there are no firm outer boundaries, centered-set organizations can feel chaotic and disorderly. Let's be honest. Some people prefer fences. They like a clear line to say who is in and who is out. It can feel better to have some firm guidelines. It is harder to find order in chaos.

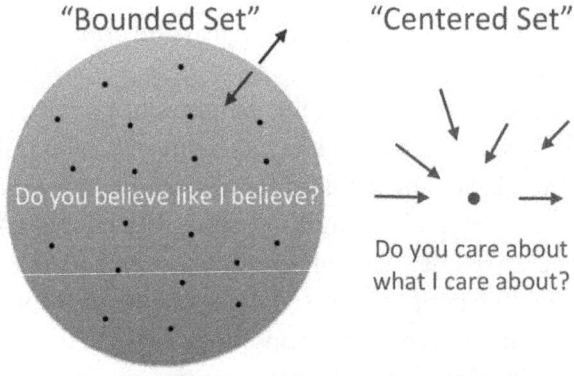

FIGURE 3

Some religious movements are beginning to understand God as a centered-set, forever creating and embracing out of love and pulling the creation into the center. Most humans are different. We can be more like a bounded set, hunched over, grabbing, and clinging. We protect what we think belongs to us and form boundaries to keep out those who scare us or who are too different from us. We have all been on the outside of a bounded set. We have been told that we lack a certain something for entrance to the get-together:

---

100 "Marks of the Church," *Next Reformation*, http://nextreformation.com/?p=1435.

We are too young or too old, too ugly or too pretty, the wrong gender, the wrong sexual identity, the wrong race, the wrong political party. We went to the wrong school or lived in the wrong place. We did not have enough money or did not belong to the right club or organization. We were not smart enough or educated enough.

Nearly all of us know what it feels like to be out. A community of grace is different, reaching wide across all lines and boundaries and pulling us into the center to organize us into a new set, a new group.

As we explore this idea, let's think again about healing in the Christian Gospels. When Jesus walked the earth, there were all kinds of healers who would make money by going from town to town casting out demons for a fee. Traveling exorcists commonly performed before sensation-seeking crowds. At first, it probably looked like Jesus was another one of these faith healers. The crowds watching Jesus would expect to be entertained, astounded and amazed by the wonder-working miracle show of Jesus of Nazareth.

Jesus changed the geography of power. Traveling exorcists who healed others for money were in it to become wealthier at the expense of another's pain. They "healed" to enlarge their egos and their pockets. Jesus could have been tempted by this. He could have given the crowds a good show and become a famous faith healer. Instead, Jesus took time to pray alone and re-focus his mission. He did not come to build his own empire. He came to topple one. Jesus came to establish a new government built on human wholeness, justice, and compassion. Roman rule was destructive emotionally and physically to people in Judea. Despite Rome's earlier tolerance of Jewish religious life, subjection to Roman rule demanded a break with Jewish religious traditions. Jesus came to re-direct these realities. His healings were not just random acts of charity. Healings were not side show spectacles to make quick money. Healings were his way of showing that God demands human well-being, even in the face of death.

The renewal of our society, the re-making of our communities, and the healing of our warring world will come neither through a recovery of doctrine, nor through innovative projects of evangelism; neither through social action, nor elegant sermons. Neither will healing renewal come about by believing, behaving or belonging. Open-set communities will come about by *becoming* ... becoming communities of grace rather than communities of condemnation.

Spiritual activists call us to become the people who share grace instead of those who think we get to decide who is in and who is outside of the circle love. Spiritual activists call us to become spiritual beings who live grounded, balanced lives. Spiritual activists call us to become those who can expand the circle of our tribe to include not just our family, our friends, our nation, but all sentient beings everywhere.

Spiritual activists call our communities to become the protesters, the revolutionaries, the peacemakers, the prophets, the teachers, the leaders, the holy provocateurs, the healers who refuse to let unjust systems of oppression have the last word. Open-set communities will come about as we learn to become those whose common life bears these marks of love.

For Conversation

- In what ways does your faith community exhibit the qualities of a bounded-set organization?
- In what ways does your faith community exhibit the qualities of a centered-set organization?
- Tell a story about a time when your spiritual activism demonstrated qualities of believing, belonging, behaving, and becoming.

For Active Contemplation: Lectio Divina on Hebrews 13:1-2

> *Let mutual love continue. Do not neglect to show hospitality to a stranger, for by doing that some have entertained angels without knowing it.* Hebrews 13: 1-2

Read this passage three times, slowly, meditatively, and expectantly. Each time you read it, pause for a moment of silence. We will ask three different sets of questions of the scripture after each period of reading and rest or silence. Then we will ruminate and reflect on a question and offer a chance to respond.

- **Cycle One:** Read, Rest, then Ruminate: What one word or phrase sticks out, or touches your heart? Respond: Be curious. What is going on in your spirit that might cause that word to catch your eye?
- **Cycle Two:** Read, Rest, then Ruminate: What personal struggle or longing is God speaking into? Respond: Feel the struggle or longing. Breathe into it. You do not have to fix it right now. Be aware.
- **Cycle Three:** Read, Rest, then Ruminate: Receive what the Spirit wants for you today. Respond: What is your personal invitation? In what ways do you sense God inviting you to act on what you experienced?

For Contemplative Action

The work of spiritual activism does not lie so much in what we do as it lies in the love with which we do it. Consider forming a centered-set community contemplative prayer sitting on a regular basis. This would be an open-invitation, non-judgmental space for people in the wider community to practice loving, active contemplation together. Pair the prayer time with Conversation of how the Divine is at work in those gathered. Seek to make the group a diverse assembly of ages, genders, classes, and religious affiliations.

13

Faith Is a Verb

A faith of convenience is a hollow faith. ~ Father Mulcahy, M*A*S*H

I once worked as a chaplain in a Boston hospital, visiting various patients on my roster. One woman's face remains with all these years later. I do not remember her name anymore, but I remember her face. She was an older adult sitting in a gloomy hospital room with the curtains drawn, staring at the floor through thick, goggle-like eyeglasses that made her eyes look comically large. There were no lights on. There were no get-well cards in the room, no flowers, no music, no indication that anyone cared she was there. As we chatted, she said that her only child, a son, did not talk to her anymore. As her body failed slowly, she was convinced she had done something wrong and was forsaken by her family and her God. She had a question for me: "Why doesn't God heal me? I've asked for forgiveness. I've tried to do the right thing. I have faith. I pray and pray, but I don't get better. I once heard a minister say if I have enough faith, God will answer my prayers. What more can I do?" And she began to sob in the dark corner of her hospital room.

I have met many people like her since that encounter in the hospital; people who suffer in sorrow because they believe something about God's miraculous power that just does not square with their experience. We have all heard a convincing clergy person, an earnest friend, or a bestselling book proclaim, "If you only have enough faith, you will have complete physical healing. If you only have enough faith you will experience financial recovery. If you only have enough faith, your relationships will flourish." Those statements put the responsibility squarely on the shoulders of the sufferer. It must be *your* fault God does not grant your heart's desire. If you are not living a healthy, prosperous life, then *you* are doing something wrong. If you need a healing, you cannot sit back and wait for God to drop it down on you. You must do whatever it takes to claim the blessing that rightfully belongs to you.

Faith that can be quantified "enough" or "not enough" sounds suspect.

What is this faith? For some, the definition of faith goes something like this: "Faith is believing the unseen as the truth. Faith is hoping for, expecting and holding on to something for which there is no proof." The problem with this definition is that it sets up a system of haves and have-nots, insiders and outsiders, those who get something from God and those who do not. The underlying assumption is those who have enough belief in God's unseen power and miraculous promises receive blessing. If God is not blessing you, then you do not believe correctly. Faith becomes a matter of pursuing personal happiness, almost as if it is an inalienable right. This way of thinking justifies the disease of unchecked individualism, which experiences faith as a matter of personal belief rather than community action.

Is that what the common good is for, to ensure individual happiness and prosperity for the believer? This definition of faith runs counter to the values of spiritual activists who work to mend the torn fabric of humanity, reestablish created goodness, and care for both the relationships that are most in need of healing and the people who are most in need of care.

Let's explore a different definition of faith that offers freedom instead of guilt. Consider this text from the Christian New Testament.

> *After Jesus had finished all his sayings in the hearing of the people, he entered Capernaum. A centurion there had a slave whom he valued highly, and who was ill and close to death. When he heard about Jesus, he sent some Jewish elders to him, asking him*

The Space Between 113

to come and heal his slave. When they came to Jesus, they appealed to him earnestly, saying, "He is worthy of having you do this for him, for he loves our people, and it is he who built our synagogue for us." And Jesus went with them, but when he was not far from the house, the centurion sent friends to say to him, "Lord, do not trouble yourself, for I am not worthy to have you come under my roof; therefore I did not presume to come to you. But only speak the word, and let my servant be healed. For I also am a man set under authority, with soldiers under me; and I say to one, 'Go,' and he goes, and to another, 'Come,' and he comes, and to my slave, 'Do this,' and the slave does it." When Jesus heard this he was amazed at him, and turning to the crowd that followed him, he said, "I tell you, not even in Israel have I found such faith." When those who had been sent returned to the house, they found the slave in good health. Luke 7:1-10

The Gospel of Luke often puts Jesus in encounters with outcasts to make a point. For instance, in Luke's very next story in chapter 7, Jesus visits a widow and raises her dead son to life with a touch. The widow is a social pariah. Touching dead people defies the purity laws of the time. That does not stop Jesus. He raises and restores both the widow and her son to new life. He eats with sinners and tax collectors. He cures people with diseases and plagues and evil spirits. In Luke 7:1-0, the outsider is a Roman Centurion, a warrior. He represents the worst of what Roman occupation offers. Centurions launch spears and javelins with strength and agility. They have expert knowledge in how to fight with sword and shield. The popular perception of many centurions was that they were brawny, not too brainy, and often abusive.[101] Here we have a

---

101 Vegetius was an historian from the 5th century, the period of the late Roman Empire, who wrote a book called *The Epitome of Military Science*. In it, he described the qualities of a centurion in rather glowing terms. "A centurion is chosen for great strength and tall stature, as a man who hurls spears and javelins skillfully and strongly, has expert knowledge how to fight with the sword and rotate the shield, and has learned the whole art of armature. He is alert, sober, and agile, and more ready to do the things ordered of him than speak, keeps his soldiers in training, makes them practice their arms, and sees that they are well clothed and shod, and that

Roman soldier, the backbone of the Roman army, displaying faith in Jesus. Jesus says he has never seen anything like it. But what is *it*, really? Is the Centurion's faith courageous hope in a reality with no proof, or is something else going on here?

The Greek word for faith used here is *pistis*. For you philosophers out there, it is the same word from which we get epistemology. The original Pistis was one of the good spirits who escaped Pandora's Box and fled back to heaven abandoning humankind. Pistis, along with the other good spirits, deserted the earth and left humanity to be overrun by evil hungers. In this context, the original meaning of *pistis* meant, "trust in others." *Pistis* does not mean belief. It means *trust*. Faith is a verb. Perhaps, instead of thinking about faith as a static concept, spiritual activists can think about faith as contemplative action. We could call it "faithing," to use a term coined by a Baptist clergy colleague, Rev. Robert Tiller. He says faithing means trying to find God in the daily activities of life and to give thanks for the love of God in my life. Faithing means trying to follow the example and teachings of Jesus and trying to grow in discipleship. Faithing means living each day with values that embrace the goodness and holiness of all creation, values that may be quite different from some people around us. Faithing means pursuing peace, justice and love for all creation and sensing God's Spirit joining us in that pursuit. Faithing means realizing that today I may have real doubts about God, and tomorrow I may again have real doubts, but God still loves me. Faithing is seeing God's presence in every person on the planet. Faithing means trying to pray even when I find it very difficult to do so. Faithing means appreciating the goodness of life each day and giving thanks for it. Faithing means realizing that God's spirit works in and through other religions, not just our own. Faithing means trusting that the power and source of the universe is good. Faithing means trying hard to rely with

---

the arms are burnished and bright" Vegetius, *Epitome of Military Science*, quoted by Alyce M. McKenzie, "The Faith of a Soldier: Reflections on Luke 7:1-10," *Patheos* (May 26, 2013), http://www.patheos.com/Progressive-Christian/Faith-Soldier-Alyce-McKenzie-05-27-2013.

confidence on God's love, even my soul is parched. Each day I am faithing as best I can, that is, trying to live by faith. Faith as a verb opens us to the possibility of a world renewed by love. It has the power to move an outsider to compassion and to trust restorative power. We can leverage our power to control others through fear and domination, or we can leverage our power to repair the word.[102]

In a world of indifference to those on the margins, we find the trust to pay attention. When people in power turn to violence and anger to solve problems, we find the trust to be peacemakers. When our loved-ones struggle with invisible pain, we find the trust to be communities of embrace. When beauty is hidden, we find the trust to marvel at the treasures the universe created each of us to be. When equality is compromised; when fear threatens to separate us; when it looks like faith, restraint, and charity have flown into the heavens and left humanity to suffer at its own hands; we find the trust, as communities of love and hope, to help restore the fractures of the world. We work a day at a time, an act at a time, for as long as it takes to make our communities places of justice and compassion where the lonely are not alone and the poor are not without help, where the cry of the vulnerable is heeded and those who are wronged are heard.

One more thing: While faithing has a strong individual dimension, it is best done in community. We support each other in our faithing. We get through rough patches together, we clarify with each other what it means to live with integrity, we talk about God together, we seek to interpret the Bible together, we work for justice together, we hold one another in sadness and grief, we forgive one another for hurts, we encourage each other in multiple ways.

---

102 From a sermon by Rev. Robert Tiller at Christ Congregational Church, August 23, 2015 <http://www.cccsilverspring.org/sermons / sermon-for-august-23-2015?rq=tiller >.

For Conversation

- Think of a time in your spiritual journey when you expressed faith as trusting action, as opposed to belief in the unseen. Find a way to express that story and share it with others.
- How might the concept of "faithing" release us from guilt and shame?
- Instead of thinking about belonging to a "faith" community, think about belonging to, behaving as, and believing like a "faithing" community. How does this shift in language, an addition of three letters, change how your worship community does mission and service?

For Active Contemplation

Faith disconnected from real life and real suffering is vanity. And vanity is a luxury that spiritual activists can no longer afford in today's world. Think of a time when you felt a disconnection between your faith and life events. How did you recognize that disconnection? How did you feel? Consider this poem by the mystic Kabir. He lived around the year 1500 CE. Kabir was a Muslim who tried to reconcile Sufi Islam with Hinduism. He wanted people to leave aside the Qur'an and Vedas, and people's entrenched assumptions, so they could follow the simple way of oneness with God. Here is one of his poems, translated by Robert Bly:

> *Friend, hope for the guest while you are alive.*
> *Jump into experience while you are alive!*
> *Think . . . and think . . . while you are alive.*
> *What you call salvation belongs to the time before death.*
> *If you don't break your ropes while you are alive,*
> *Do you think ghosts will do it after?*
> *The idea that the soul will rejoin with the ecstatic just because*
> *the body is rotten—*
> *That is all fantasy.*
> *What is found now is found then.*
> *If you find nothing now,*

> *You will simply end up with an apartment in the City of Death.*
> *If you make love with the divine now,*
> *In the next life you will have the face of satisfied desire.*
> *So plunge into the truth, find out who the Teacher is.*
> *Believe in the Great Sound!*
> *Kabir says this:*
> *When the Guest is being searched for,*
> *It is the intensity of the longing for the Guest that does all the work.*
> *Look at me, and you will see a slave of that intensity.*[103]

Where do you experience glimpses and little reminders of the reality of *now*? For some, it is in the simplest treasures: A supporting hand upon a shoulder or a loving brush of the cheek; the softest whisper of truth spoken in adoration; the early morning orchestra of music from the birds outside the window; the refreshment of the breeze, the contagious laughter of those we love; the pain of loss; the miracle of healing; the unstoppable toil for a better world; the constant reminders of how precious each moment truly is; and the moments when we experience kindness and compassion. As we become present to ourselves and God and others, we begin a journey without end. All we are asked to do is start down that road.

Meditate on the reality of *now* as you close your eyes. Focus on tensing and relaxing each muscle group for two to three seconds each. Start with the feet and toes, then move up to the knees, thighs, rear, chest, arms, hands, neck, jaw and eyes — all while maintaining deep, slow breaths. Try this method: breathe in through the nose, hold for a count of five while the muscles tense, then breathe out through the mouth on release.

FOR CONTEMPLATIVE ACTION

Many New Testament scholars contend that we can learn more about the Jesus of the scriptures from the things that he does rather than from the words that he speaks. The Jesus we meet in

---

[103] Robert Bly, *The Kabir Book: Forty-four of the Ecstatic Poems of Kabir* (Boston: Beacon Press, 1977), 24.

the gospels is a man of action. He heals. He forgives. He demonstrates compassion. He takes a stand against injustices. He shares. He weeps. He loves unconditionally. He then tells his disciples and interested followers to go and do likewise. Maybe that is why the writers of all three synoptic gospels wrote that Jesus believed that the most important commandment is to "love God with all your heart, soul, and mind and to love your neighbor as yourself." What challenges might arise in a church community that requires no dogmatic beliefs? Create a list of behaviors that you think are reflections of your worship community's faith, as it stands today.

14

The Death of False Hope

> Hope deferred makes the heart sick, but a desire fulfilled is a tree of life. ~ Proverbs 13:12

Can you remember a time when you lost hope, a time when you thought that life would not get better, or a time when you chose to run rather than weep because you did not want to get involved? As a minister, I attend the bedsides of those who die slowly of debilitating illnesses. Sometimes I visit homes or hospital rooms daily. Although my visits are brief, I listen to family members who live in the presence of gradual death, day in and day out, with little or no breathing space of their own. Over time and many visits, I can see different reactions to those who are dying.

Some caregivers lose hope because they know their situation is truly hopeless. There are no remedies or cures to sustain hope anymore. For some, hope is a curse. In our conversation on faith in the previous chapter, we noted that *Pistis* was one of the good spirits who fled from Pandora's Box. As spirits flew from the box to either leave or torment the human world, Pandora slammed the lid shut just in time to keep the most evil spirit from escaping. The evil spirit's name was Hope. Friedrich Nietzsche picked up on this detail when he wrote,

> Pandora brought the box of ills and opened it. It was the gift of the gods to men, outwardly a beautiful and seductive gift, and called the Casket of Happiness. Out of it flew all the evils, living winged creatures, thence they now circulate and do Men injury day and night. One single evil had not yet escaped

from the box, and by the will of Zeus, Pandora closed the lid and it remained within. Now for ever Man has the casket of happiness in his house and thinks he holds a great treasure; it is at his disposal, he stretches out his hand for it whenever he desires; for he does not know the box which Pandora brought was the casket of evil, and he believes the ill which remains within to be the greatest blessing, it is hope. Zeus did not wish Man, however much he might be tormented by the other evils, to fling away his life, but to go on letting himself be tormented again and again. Therefore he gives Man hope -- in reality it is the worst of all evils, because it prolongs the torments of Man.[104]

Dante picked up on this idea in *The Divine Comedy* when Virgil led him to the gates of the Inferno, over which were inscribed, "All hope abandon ye who enter here." It is pointless to waste time on hope when one is about to become a permanent resident of Hell.

Some caregivers use protective emotional strategies to shield themselves from overwhelming sorrow. Sometimes they joke. Sometimes they clean. Sometimes they do things that do not necessarily need to be done for the patient, but which give the caregiver the sense of helping. Sometimes, in the middle of a conversation, you can sense that a sorrow-soaked family member is not there in the moment. The caretaker shuts it all out. Hope is too painful. I think of this when I read the poem that many people consider to be Emily Dickinson's homage to optimism, " 'Hope' is the thing with feathers."

> *"Hope" is the thing with feathers –*
> *That perches in the soul –*
> *And sings the tune without the words –*
> *And never stops – at all –*

---

[104] Friedrich Nietzsche, *Human All Too Human: a Book for Free Spirits*, first published in 1878, Lexido.com, <http://www.lexido.com/EBOOK_TEXTS/HUMAN_ALL_TOO_HUMAN_BOOK_ONE_.aspx?S=71>. Emphasis added.

> *And sweetest – in the Gale – is heard –*
> *And sore must be the storm –*
> *That could abash the little Bird*
> *That kept so many warm –*
>
> *I've heard it in the chillest land –*
> *And on the strangest Sea –*
> *Yet – never – in Extremity,*
> *It asked a crumb – of me.*[105]

Notice how "Hope" has quotation marks around it. If we were listening to the poem being read aloud, the speaker might lift fingers in the air and make bunny-eared, air-quote hand gestures to let us know that Dickinson exaggerates and calls attention to the word "hope" to move us beyond our conventional understanding. The ceaseless, sweet singing bird never asks anything of the poet, except to keep on listening and hoping during the tempest. Such brightness in the face of horror can be a burden, not a gift. Spiritual values like faith, hope, and love always require active response on our part. To remain passively optimistic, so hopeful that everything will be all right when clearly it is not, can be naïve at best, and heartlessly callous at its worst

Knowing how hard it can be to sustain hope, some people will limit hope by becoming emotionally militant. Consider the mock-Latin aphorism: *Illegitimi non carborundum*. The phrase means something like, "Don't let the illegitimate ones grind you down." Coined in World War II, Barry Goldwater picked it up in the 1960s. These words reportedly sat prominently on the desk the former Speaker of the House, John Boehner. At first glance, *Illegitimi non carborundum* has some appeal. The phrase is assertive. It says, "Hope is for the weak. I am going to be tough in the face of despair. I will not let those who suffer pull me down. I will re-

---

[105] Emily Dickinson, " 'Hope is the things with feathers," The Poetry Foundation, quoted from *The Poems of Emily Dickinson* R. W. Franklin, ed., (Harvard University Press, 1999), https://www.poetryfoundation.org/poems-and-poets/poems/detail/42889.

sist."[106] It sounds hard-hitting and muscular, but is it true? When we deny suffering we may take on even more suffering. I remember times when I have chosen to run rather than weep because I did not want to even hope that things could get better. It is all too easy to look the other way and abandon hope when it feels like the world around us is crumbling to ashes in our human-made hells. When denial does not work, when protective emotional strategies do not help us, when anger and stoicism cause more suffering, what are we to do? Although humans appear to be creatures who can anticipate a better world, we are also are creatures so wounded and battered that we can give in to despair. "Hope" alone is not enough to fix the unjust structures that cause ruin, rubble, horror and unimaginable suffering. "Hope" alone is not enough to help us understand our complicity with and resistance to the powers and principalities that hold sway over our organizations and institutions. At its worst, "Hope" sits on our shoulders and chirps a bright lullaby while we watch horror after horror on our TV screens and Internet news feeds.

I write this knowing full well that hope is a cornerstone of Christian religious experience, rooted in a theology of a heavenly utopia for those who are faithful to the Kingdom of Christ. Instead of abandoning or deferring hope as suggested in Proverbs 13:12, we need to differentiate between false hope and realistic hope. False hope is Dickinson's "Hope" in quotes. It is what Ernst Bloch, often called the philosopher of hope, criticized as abstract utopian thinking. *False hope* is expressed in dreams without any trace of possibility for breaking into history. False hope is wishful thinking without the will to change anything. It focuses only on fantasy and memory.

A mainline, urban church hired a congregational consultant to help revitalize itself. Through a series of one-on-one and group interviews, the consultant asked members of the congregation to

---

[106] William C. Pender, "Giving Up Something Bad for Lent" (3/9/2014), First Presbyterian Church of Knoxville, http://www.fpcknox.org/site/wp-content/uploads/2014/03/Sermon-3-9-2014-Pender.pdf.

describe their dream of the future of their church. When I asked the consultant what the church members said, he replied, "It was so interesting. Most members spent their interview time describing the great things they did 25 or 50 years ago. They want it all to happen again. They don't realize that those memories cannot be recreated in the future." False hope wants people to believe the glories of the past are the possibilities of the future, even though all evidence points to the contrary.

Realistic hope can be equated with what Bloch called concrete utopian thinking. Instead of being bound in a fantasy of the past, realistic hope reaches forward towards actual possibility with both wishful and willful thinking. It focuses on what can really be achieved.[107]

The congregational consultant just mentioned worked with the church to form realistic expectations of what is possible based on demographics, their current resources, and an appropriate amount of challenge. Members of the church still dream of being a resilient, more pliable church, but their dream is based on what can be achieved, given the current climate.

Relinquishing false hope can be a process of recovery. Like any process of relinquishment, letting go can trigger grief, lament, and tears. Whenever we are stirred to such depths, these may be times God is working in our lives. Check the times and places where you weep, and you might feel the places where God wants to get through to you. We learn that such deep emotions open us God's care. God pieces together something real when we let go of false, abstract utopias.

The story of Lazarus as told in the Gospel of John reminds me of the abandonment of false hope.

> *Now a certain man was ill, Lazarus of Bethany, the village of Mary and her sister Martha. Mary was the one who anointed the Lord with perfume and wiped his feet with her hair; her brother*

---

107 Ruth Levitas, "Educated Hope: Ernst Bloch on Abstract and Concrete Utopias," *Not Yet; Reconsidering Ernst Bloch*, Jamie Owen Daniel and Tom Moylan, eds. (London: Verso, 1997), 65-68.

Lazarus was ill. So the sisters sent a message to Jesus, "Lord, he whom you love is ill." But when Jesus heard it, he said, "This illness does not lead to death; rather it is for God's glory, so that the Son of God may be glorified through it." Accordingly, though Jesus loved Martha and her sister and Lazarus, after having heard that Lazarus was ill, he stayed two days longer in the place where he was. John 11:1-6

Jesus knows his friend is on the point of death, and lingers intentionally for two days before travelling to Bethany. He insists that Lazarus will not die. Jesus finally arrives on the scene, but he is too late. Lazarus is dead. Three nights dead. By now, everyone has given up hope. No happy ending. No miracle. No beautiful finale. It is too late. Jesus weeps. I am sure there is some denial. Some anger. Some bargaining. Some emotional protective strategies to shield mourners from overwhelming sorrow.

Why did Jesus wait so long? I wonder if it had to do with the death of false hope. Did Jesus wait because the disciples and the people mourning at Lazarus' tomb all needed to do some soul work? Maybe they required the time to slow down enough to wonder about God. Perhaps it offered a chance to give up on hollow words of hope, and to let the trite, empty phrases we hear at a death run their course. We have all heard, "He is in a better place now. God called him home. God must have had a reason to let him die. Don't worry, you will get over it." These phrases, while meant to offer comfort, can fill mourners with shame and self-doubt. They lack compassion. "Hope" isolated from compassion is treacherous and destructive. Condolence is of little value if it is not guided by realistic hope that can transform comfort into compassion.

Then Jesus calls out a name and a command. "Lazarus! Get up!" Through tears of sadness and the torment of false hope, Jesus calls his name. In the face of anger and denial and stoicism, in the face of skepticism and lament, Lazarus walks out of the stony portico of a garden tomb. Finally, everyone understands the meaning of the name Lazarus', which means, "God has helped." On the fourth hopeless day, God has helped.

In the darkness of ruined relationships, in frustrating and unsuccessful attempts to make our bruised world better, in failed dreams of beauty and happy endings, in the entombed hopeless reality of life's shadows, our religious traditions affirm a special, divine voice calling your name. Through the tears and the torment of false hope the Spirit breaks through the craggy veneer of hardness behind which we entomb ourselves and says, "God has helped! Now rise." When we wonder if anybody cares, the tears of Jesus remind us that God cares. God understands when and how it hurts. When life shatters, go ahead and weep with sadness. God helps us pick up the pieces and makes something out of what is left. God cares about you. Weep with realistic hope.

For Conversation

- What do you think about this statement: " 'Hope' alone is not enough to fix the unjust structures that cause ruin, rubble, horror and unimaginable suffering"?
- Think about a time you have wept with realistic hope. Did hope cause more suffering? Did hope promote some new action?

For Active Contemplation

Writing for *Sojourners*, Lauren Carlson says without contemplation hope is stagnant, but hope that partners with contemplation activates transformation. She reminds us,

> When collectively we are at our worst, let us look back at what we've overcome — and remember our deep connection to one another into the future. Contemplative practice is the figurative room in which we experience the freedom to remember and courage to respond. It is what it means to have hope as a spiritual practice.[108]

---

[108] Lauren K. Carlson, "Room for Hope: Why Justice Work Needs Contemplation," *Sojourners* (Oct. 12, 2016), https://sojo.net/articles/room-hope-why-social-justice-needs-contemplation.

In your prayer practice, what does it mean to have realistic hope?

For Contemplative Action: Music of Hope

Think about music as an instrument of survival and protest for Black Americans since slavery. Creating jazz and blues music in America was a process of protest and resistance. When Dr. King marched on Washington, DC in 1963, the legacy was not only his "I Have a Dream Speech," but also the freedom songs that carried over from the Montgomery Bus Boycott. People endured torture by Whites by singing songs together. Music provided comfort and courage. The song with the most force was "We Shall Overcome." Music's effectiveness, whether the songs were the blues or soul, reggae or Afro-beat, funk or some new fusion, seems connected to the collective and individual experiences of Black people. The music that projects those experiences with intensity and power is the music that people will relate to and identify with.[109]

What songs give your faith community a sense of realistic hope and energy? What resonates? What music gives you comfort and courage in the struggle for justice? Come up with a list of styles and song titles that galvanize your faith community and help move you to resist hatred with realistic hope?

---

109 Eddie Yancey, "Rhythm and Blues protest songs: voices of resistance," *ETD Collection* for AUC Robert W. Woodruff Library, Paper 610, (Atlanta: Clark Atlanta University, 2007), 34-36.

15

LOVE: THE CONNECTIVE CURRENT OF LIFE

Dear friends, let us continue to love one another, for love comes from God. Anyone who loves is a child of God and knows God. But anyone who does not love does not know God, for God is love. God showed how much he loved us by sending his one and only Son into the world so that we might have eternal life through him. This is real love -- not that we loved God, but that he loved us and sent his Son as a sacrifice to take away our sins. Dear friends, since God loved us that much, we surely ought to love each other. No one has ever seen God. But if we love each other, God lives in us, and God's love is brought to full expression in us. And God has given us his Spirit as proof that we live in him and he in us. ~ 1 John 4:7-13

How do you define yourself? I am a married, White, straight, educated, 40-ish-year-old child of the '80s with four children, who enjoys variety in my menu, who likes to dress in mismatched plaids, and enjoys a relatively good amount of health and happiness. You could say something similar about yourself. Each of these descriptions is a code to more understanding. When I was born, what I eat, how I dress, how much money I make, where I live and with whom – you form assumptions based on what you see and hear about me.

I am also more than any of that. I am defined by my consciousness. I think. I evaluate. I act on decisions. I am aware of my world. However, I do not always know why I do the things I do, so something else must be at work.

Am I defined by my sub-conscious? Sometimes I sense unknown motives and desires behind what I do. How can I explain an urge to suddenly call an old friend or to take a drive alone? How can I put in plain words why I want to cross my legs when I sit down? Sometimes we can find triggers for our impulses, but usually we just move from one subconscious impulse to another without any real awareness of why we do what we do. I know there are two parts of me, conscious and subconscious. But I do not know enough about these parts and how they work to form a good picture of who I am.

There is a spiritual me, driven by unseen forces and universal realities that are bigger than I can fathom. There is the me that others see. People have an opinion about me when they get to know me. Am I any of this? Can I know the real me? Can you know the real me?

When people try to explain that which is difficult to put to words, we use two different kinds of languages. We can call them Day Language and Night Language – two different but complimentary sides of our experience.

Day Language is the realm of objective reality. Day Language talks about what is empirically true. In Day Language terms, I can explain that the average 150 lb. adult human body contains approximately 6.7×1027 atoms and is composed of 60 chemical elements, although only 24 or 25 of those elements are thought to play an active positive role in human life and growth. There are about 210 distinct human cell types. There are between 50 and 75 trillion cells in the human body. Each of those cells contains thousands of protein molecules.

There is another reality, communicated to us through dreams, poems, metaphors and stories. It communicates a subjective reality. It wants to be interpreted. Let's call this Night Language. I can say I am fearfully and wonderfully made. I am a child of God. God leads me to green pastures and beside still waters. I believe these things to be true, but I cannot prove them with the scientific method.

We need both Day Language and Night Language to better understand who we are. Consider this biblical image: "You are dust and to dust you shall return." What does this mean? Well, it turns out that the elements that make up my body are also part of the earth's crust. We are dust. Or, instead of earth dust, we can think of ourselves as star dust. The elements in the earth's crust had to come from somewhere. Our atoms were created from supernova explosions of distant stars, blown out in stellar winds from massive detonations that soared for millions of years through space to become part of the birth of our solar system. Our bodies have billions of bits of cosmic information that have been encoded and preserved in each of us, stored right in our bodies. We are dust, of the day and of the night. We are connected to the earth and the cosmos in love. We use Day Language to seek clarity with measurable facts, and then we express our understanding in the poetry and stories of Night Language. You are earth dust, connected elementally to the earth as its grandest expression. You are a star child, an expression of the blazing light and explosive power of the sun.

Perhaps this is how we begin to understand the love of God – the evolving, breathing, life-giving connection that unites us. We need Day Language and Night Language to understand the fundamental affirmation of our Scripture: God is love. Far from being removed from the world, God is in every single atom of the cosmos, including you.

Both science and spirituality are beginning to affirm there are connections between everything in the universe that we can no longer afford to ignore. A biologist named Rupert Sheldrake created a controversial concept called morphic fields. Sheldrake claims each individual both draws upon and contributes to the collective memory of the species. This means that new patterns of behavior can spread more rapidly than would otherwise be possible. For example, if rats of a certain breed learn a new trick in a university laboratory, then rats of that breed should be able to learn the same trick faster all over the world. If enough chimpanzees learned to ride a bike, then it should be easier for the entire species to learn, no matter where they live. Habits are subject to natural selection; and the more often they are repeated, the more probable they become, other things being equal. Animals, including humans, inherit the successful habits of their species as instincts. We collect bodily, emotional, mental and cultural habits, including the habits of our languages.[110]

In other words, we are never apart from the connective current of life. Everything is related. If humans practice violence and the habits of hatred, then it becomes easier for all humans to become disciples of death. But, if we practice love and live with compassion, if we see ourselves united with God and others, if we work for a more humane world, then we enable the entire species to do the same.

There is a branch of science and mathematics that studies what we think of as randomness called Chaos Theory. Chaos Theory suggests that the tiniest changes in one small area of the world can cause massive changes in other, distant parts of the world. In 1961, a meteorologist named Edward Lorenz worked on theoretical models on the development of tropical storms, typhoons and hurricanes. He came up with an idea called the "butterfly effect." The small eddy of wind current made by a butterfly wing can change the weather on the other side of the globe. One small change leads to a larger change, which leads to an even larger change, and so on. Of course, if a butterfly fluttering by can add to a hurricane, more butterflies fluttering by can change the course of that hurricane entirely. In the same way, can initial small acts of kindness performed by spiritual activists also cause small changes that ripple out and eventually change the world?

In spiritual terms, let's call it the Theory of Mutuality. The actions of one influence all. The Theory of Mutuality reaches into the subatomic level of our universe. For instance, we now know that once two electrons have connected or touched in some way, they can never be the same again. No matter how far apart those

---

110 See Rupert Sheldrake, *The Presence of the Past: Morphic Resonance and the Habits of Nature* (London: Icon, 2011).

electrons go, what happens to one happens to the other. We inhabit a universe where everything is part of everything else. This is hard for some people to accept, especially in institutional churches. Most Christian church-goers were not brought up in congregations known for adaptability. Religious institutions have been known for their ability to control, restrict, contain, narrow, purify, define, and restrain. It is human nature, really. We expect people to conform to our image. We want others to dress a certain way, to behave in predictable ways, and to talk in acceptable ways. Our desire to control can get out of control. Left unchecked, people sometimes try to dominate or marginalize others. We create insiders and outsiders.

Old habits die hard, especially for entrenched religious organizations. Instead of trying to control others and make them conform to our expectations, spiritual activists submit to the collective subconscious of the community to better fulfill its mission. The Theory of Mutuality means acting individually and instinctively while giving ourselves the freedom to let others do the same.

Scientists who study the group behavior of ants, bees, locusts, schools of fish, and crowds of people are learning that swarms and crowds organize around some simple rules. Each individual member of a swarm, acting individually, will impact the behavior of others. The actions of a few members of the group affect the actions of all. No one tells the group what to do. There are no orders or commands from the leader at the top. Groups organize spontaneously, following simple, basic rules. One key to an ant colony, for example, is that no one is in charge. No generals command submissive ant warriors. No ant boss manages the ant workers. The queen plays no role except to lay eggs. Even with half a million ants, a colony functions just fine with no top-down management at all, at least none that we would recognize.

Or consider bees. What commands a hive of bees to swarm? Scientists know it is not the queen bee. When a swarm pours itself out through the front slot of the hive, the queen bee can only follow. By choice of the citizens, the swarm takes the queen and thunders off in the direction indicated by mob vote. The hive commands. The queen follows. Thousands of bees united into one collective direct themselves to swarm. The Queen Bee is not the leader. In fact, there are anonymous leaders within the swarm called "streakers." They direct from within the swarm by flying faster and straighter than the other bees. The swarm has no center, but rather thousands of autonomous individual bees engaged in parallel actions, interacting with one another and influencing each other.[111]

Science confirms something that some religions have taught for centuries – the benefit of losing the ego and becoming a part of something bigger than one's self. Relationship, connectivity, interactivity, teamwork, and mutuality: these are the processes by which every living thing is created, survives, and prospers. Almost any group that follows bees' rules will make itself smarter, whether it is investors in the stock market, scientists on a research project, kids guessing the number of jelly beans in a jar, or religious and community organizations that want to make the world a more humane and compassionate place. It turns out the group is smarter than the individual, under certain parameters. A group will not be smart if its members imitate one another, mindlessly follow fads, or wait for someone to tell them what to do. When a group is being intelligent, whether it is made up of ants or abbots, it relies on its members to do their own part.

The Theory of Mutuality is less about controlling people than releasing them. Each person must be given decision-making power to claim one's own power. Every person must be treated with dignity and respect. Mutuality helps us add complexity and diversity.

---

111   Peter Miller, "Swarm Theory," *National Geographic Magazine* (July 1, 2007), http://ngm.nationalgeographic.com/2007/07/swarms/miller-text.

Peter Miller, *The Smart Swarm: How Understanding Flocks, Schools, and Colonies Can Make Us Better at Communicating, Decision Making, and Getting Things Done* (New York: Avery, 2010).

Len Fisher, *The Perfect Swarm: The Science of Complexity in Everyday Life* (New York: Basic Books, 2009).

And we trust that diversity brings health. Therefore, spiritual activists find those who are pushed to the margins, or have less power, and invite them to relocate in the center of the action.

There is a difference between inviting the rejected into your circle and inviting them to help lead it. Perhaps you have heard faith leaders say, "God loves you just the way you are — but too much to let you stay that way." In a spirit of mutuality, spiritual activists say, "We love you just the way you are. That is all. Nothing else to add. No pre-qualifications before you are welcomed. Now please tell us your story so we can learn from you." Spiritual activists realize that we are all in the same swarm in which all members can work independently, trusting our collective wisdom and relying on our collective compassion. Perhaps now more than ever it is beginning to dawn on us that the ways in which we define ourselves, the choices we make about the foods we eat, the clothes we wear, and the cars we drive, affect life all over the world.

Mutuality … reciprocity … connecting deeply … there is another word for these concepts in spiritual terms. Love. Love comes from God. Anyone who loves belongs to God and knows God. We are all in covenant with one another. Our covenant is between God, humans, plants, animals, skies, oceans, rivers, earth. We are all in this together. The more we begin to look around and realize the world's problems — famine, rising waters, global warming, political rifts, human trafficking, worker injustice and abuse, extinction, loss of resources, you name it — we begin to make the connection that who we are affects the world. Love is the answer. It is out of love that we were formed from the dust of the earth, and it is with love that we are given back to the earth. We are in a love covenant. If we love God, we cannot help but to love God's earth. If we love God, we cannot help but to love God's earthly creations.

Years ago, after loading my car and getting ready to go to my church, my neighbor called me over. Pointing down the street, she showed me a bird, maybe a catbird or a mockingbird, flopping around in the middle of the road. It looked like it had a broken wing. My neighbor said, "Can you move it out of the road. I'm too scared to go near it. I don't want it to get run over, but I don't want to touch it."

Mustering all my bravado, I said, "I don't want to touch it either." She looked at me. I looked at her. Then I went to look at the bird. I stood over the bird and it calmed down. I reached down, and stroked its back. The bird sat in absolute stillness, neither trying to flop around or peck at me. I pushed on its tail feathers and then, as I went to cup the bird in my hand, it gathered its energy and flew away to the relative safety of a nearby thicket. I walked away feeling such a connection with that little gray bird, as if it were my sister, as if we shared a moment. I thought of the words of William Blake:

> *To see the world in a grain of sand*
> *And heaven in a wild flower,*
> *Hold infinity in the palm of your hand*
> *And eternity in an hour.*

Think of the times you enjoyed the privilege of cupping infinity in the palm of your hand, as if it were a small, wounded gray songbird, the times you had the power of healing or destruction at your fingertips, the times when you understood your connection to the connective flow of life. What a privilege. What a joy. What a responsibility.

For Conversation

Researchers collected 171 stories of compassion experienced or witnessed in the workplace from 158 employees of a community hospital in a midsized urban area in the central United States. After categorizing the acts of compassion described in the stories, researchers measured those acts along with workplace factors such as stress, well-being, and workers' commitment to the company. The researchers found convincing evidence of large effects of seemingly small interpersonal acts such as lending an ear, extending a hand, or being present to someone in pain. These actions serve as cues that workers intuitively use to understand the kind of place where they

The Space Between

work and the kind of people they work with.[112] What internal and external cues does your faith community offer that give people a "vibe" about who you are? How do people both inside and outside your faith community understand you intuitively?

FOR ACTIVE CONTEMPLATION

To get in the mindset of small acts making a big difference, create brief, succinct, haiku-like prayers. Both poetry and prayer can remove us from our focus on daily routine and can create a different outlook. For example, consider this 4-line l poem entitled, "Will Work for Peace," written in response to the terrorist attacks in Paris on November 14, 2015:

> *Yes, pray for Paris.*
> *After your Amens, help me*
> *Knead peace for starved times.*
> *Pour some wine. Kiss life.*

I wrote this after reflecting on the activist ministry of Thomas Merton:

> *A monk and a thief*
> *Defy conventions and norms.*
> *One becomes a saint.*

Or meditate on these words crafted by someone who saw a person struggling with homelessness:

> *Bridge underpass*
> *Homeless man dozes;*
> *Happy dreams lurk*[113]

End your day by writing a holy haiku, expressing your perception with prayer and precision. How might this exercise help you become aware of the connective current of life? How does

---

112 "Small Acts of Compassion," *Beliefnet* (June, 2005), http://www.beliefnet.com/wellness/health/2005/06/small-acts-of-compassion.aspx#cHJfEchmoJekoYPx.99.

113 "Haiku Poems About Prayer," http://www.haikupoemsandpoets.com/poems/prayer_haiku_poems.

expressing your experience through poetry connect you lovingly to the deep needs of the world

For Contemplative Action

The things that really change the world, according to Chaos Theory, are the tiny movements. What small act of loving compassion can you do today? A smile? A compliment? An encouraging text? What small act of loving compassion can your faith community accomplish? Feeding someone in need? Listening deeply to stories of loss and pain? Remember, acts of love shape not just the recipient, but organizations as well. How people treat those outside of our organization set tells a lot about the people inside.

16

Concluding Thoughts

This book is not meant to offer policies for change. It is meant to inspire, to persuade, to teach, and to motivate us to explore the space between a faith agenda and progressive social movements. In the end, perhaps both movements can agree on a common vision:

- To be part of connecting communities that are united in love instead of division;
- To be part of inviting communities that give special attention to the weak and forgotten, communities that find those who have been marked as enemies and makes room for them at the table;
- To be part of fair communities where women are equal to men; where gays and straight, black, white, brown and tan celebrate diversity together; where children are cherished, and elders are respected;
- To be part of mission-focused communities that offer public space to citizens who want to organize;
- To be part of honest communities where fear is not used as a technique to manipulate others into obedience; communities where love becomes an irrevocable claim on one another;
- To be part of healing communities that seek wholeness through action and include all living beings in the ambit of our compassionate activism;

- To be part of humble communities where it is more important to love than to be right and where we hear more singing than arguing.

We stand together, blessed and broken, working hard and partnering with one another to be shepherds of peace. You dreamers and prophets, you servants and peacemakers, you wounded healers, let us dry the tears and nourish the bodies of those who live in this beautiful, terrible, wonderful world.

Appendix A:

What is a Covenant?

Covenant is a three-way agreement between God and God's people.

God promises to be faithful to us.

We promise to obey God.

We also make promise to one another, finding ways to encourage one another and hold each other accountable. Covenant is an expression of God's love as well as a call to serve and love God in faithfulness.

Covenant is a response to grace. God creates an atmosphere of trust and security in which a community can find the strength to surrender to God's will. God chooses people so that people might choose God. God gives us our identity. Even when people fail to follow their side of the covenant, there is hope – the promise of reestablishment and renewal. Covenant also brings unity. Faithfulness to God brings a promised state of vitality in matters affecting the life of God's people. Covenant brings the hope of life and renewal. Covenant becomes a summation of the best we can be. God calls us into covenant community. God personally interacts with us as a community. God's aims for the community are expressed in ideas like righteousness, devotion, and love.

For Conversation

1. Based on our conversations, what stories, images, and metaphors describe our faith community at its best?
2. What are our most cherished core values?
3. If we were to put these images and core values into a covenant statement, what would we promise to God? What behaviors would we need to commit to sustain us when we are at our best?
4. How might our faith community look and feel if we adopted these commitments as a congregation?

Creating a Group Covenant

1. Think of a story about a time when you felt, safe, nurtured and appreciated. Who are the characters? What sights, sounds and smells do you remember? How did you feel?
2. Can you identify your personal values that this story illustrates? Think of a symbol or metaphor that represents this story.

Looking for common symbols, images, and values among the group participants, write a statement of mutual commitments, stated positively, that represent how we will treat one another when we are at our best.

Appendix B:

A Sample Just Peace Covenant

We, the members of this faith community, are mindful of the history of covenantal relationships between God and God's children. We remember God's loving promise to Israel, "I will be your God and you will be my people."

We remember the fulfillment of God's promise to the exiled remnant that a Savior would be sent to teach God's vision of Shalom to those who earnestly and humbly seek to know and live that vision.

We realize that we have not always fulfilled our part of the covenant. It is often easier to remain silent before the forces of chaos and death.

Therefore, on this day we publicly and prayerfully commit ourselves to our part in God's vision by proclaiming this congregation a Just Peace Church. With God's help and by Christ's example we shall work for peace and seek justice for all peoples.

We pledge to learn more about the needs of those everywhere who have not shared in God's intention of abundant living.

We pledge continued efforts to nourish existing ties and to establish new ones with our brothers and sisters outside our own community.

We pledge greater sensitivity to and support for all the world's peoples in our shared struggles for liberation.

We pledge to promote peaceful resolutions to conflict.

We pledge to be more mindful of and responsible for the integrity of God's Creation.

We covenant to work together to establish God's Reign on earth and to seek a new world and a renewed invigorated Church established on the love demonstrated in the life of our Savior Jesus Christ.

Appendix C:

A Sample Open, Affirming, & Welcoming Covenant

Our faith community is a covenant community where all people are recognized as being made in God's image, reconciled by Christ and empowered by the Holy Spirit. We believe that gay, lesbian, bisexual, and transgender people share, with all others, worth that comes from being a unique individual loved by God. We recognize that Christians differ on issues of sexual orientation and gender identity, but our understanding of the nature of God requires us to embrace all people. Therefore, our faith community intentionally welcomes and affirms gay, lesbian, bisexual, and transgender persons to journey in faith with us.

We believe that as members of the community of faith we are called to love one another and ourselves as whole persons. We seek to relate to one another with love, trust and in ways that are mutually accountable and nurturing. Our covenant commitment challenges us to welcome all people into the life of our faith community.

We recognize the diversity of families among us and the ways in which God calls us into relationship. We support traditional and extended families, single persons and those who are widowed and divorced. We value all families, including gay, lesbian, bisexual, and transgender persons' families and seek to nurture and support the commitments they make.

We believe that God creates and celebrates diversity and declare our openness to all who seek Christ's love in our midst. We openly affirm this belief and commit ourselves to its realization in all aspects of our life together.

Appendix D:

A Sample Racial Justice Covenant

Our faith community holds a vision of becoming a multi-cultural, multi-racial, anti-racist congregation that more faithfully reflects the surrounding community. We are a covenant faith community who believe that all people are made in God's image, reconciled by Christ and empowered by the Holy Spirit. We believe it is our role to take an active stance in systematically dismantling racism. A part of an anti-racism stance is acknowledging a system of white privilege in the United States which tends to perpetuate societal stereotypes in all its citizens.

We believe that our commitment to anti-racism should be reflected in the life and culture of the congregation through our policies, programs and practices as we continue to learn about racism. We are committed to developing and working to implement strategies that dismantle racism through our adult and children's education, Sunday services, mission giving, purchases and business practices, and community outreach and action.

We believe we are all called to work against racism and work for a society in which the words of the Gospel are realized among us.

We acknowledge that our faith community has a rich heritage of engagement in addressing racism in our society over the years, and we recognize that our anti-racism journey is a continuing one.

Therefore, we claim the prophetic work and title "Covenanting to be an Anti-racist Church."

Appendix E:

A Non-Violent Communion

INVITATION

Shout joy to the Lord, all the earth,
Serve the Lord with gladness,
Enter God's presence with joy.
Indeed, the Lord is good!
God's love is forever.
Faithful from age to age.
All peoples shall remember and turn,
All nations will bow to the Lord.

Friends, this is the joyful feast of the people of God! People will come from east and west, from north and south, and will eat in the presence of God. As we come to the table, we share bread as a sign of peace and fellowship. We share the cup and embrace a new life that practices forgiveness, renounces violence and seeks the reconciliation of all people under God's love. Let us come to the Table as those who sense God's presence at work in diverse people and in surprising ways. Let us celebrate, with joy, the freely offered love of God that sustains all people, and is now embodied for us in the gifts of bread and wine.

THE GREAT THANKSGIVING

The One who was God in the beginning is with us in the bread.
The One of whom prophets spoke now speaks to us in this cup.

The One who embraces the world holds us together, surrounding all in the arms of peace.

We thank you God, for gracious, frequent, and unexpected invitations to share in divine life. When we listen to your voice in the religious traditions that surround us, we understand that your bountiful love is greater than we could ever have imagined on our own.

We follow the way of Christ. Through his life, death and resurrection, you forged a bond with us that cannot be broken. In Christ's death, you enter the depths of our sin. In his rising, you offer the assurance of a new and changed life. Therefore, we praise you, joining with all those who seek you and express their deepest praise and who forever sing the glory of your many names *(we invite worshippers to speak some of those names out loud)*.

In Jesus, we hear your Word of love. He lived as one of us, seeking us in our disjointed lives and connecting us to you and to one another in a new community. In life, he traveled beyond the borders of his country to communicate your love. He healed Gentiles and preached to Samaritans. He invited Roman soldiers, tax collectors and the marginalized of society to eat at his table. He showed us a world of inclusive wholeness, restoring people's humanity, inviting them to renounce sin and fulfill God's aims for the world. Dying on the cross, he calls us to join all people of faith who choose the path of suffering love instead of hatred and peaceful resistance instead of violence. Rising again, he calls humanity to believe that a world for God is a world transformed: A world in which the poor are fed, the homeless are sheltered, and prisoners are treated humanely; a world where we are united in our commonalities instead of excluded by our differences; a world where neither death, nor life, nor angels, nor rulers, nor things present, nor things to come, nor powers, nor height, nor depth, nor anything else in all creation, will be able to separate us one from the many expressions of love that God has for us and that we can show to one another. We praise you for the many ways that you have come to show us how all creation can be made new.

Remembering your gracious acts, we take from your creation this bread and this cup and joyfully celebrate our life together. With thanksgiving, we dedicate our lives to you.

Gracious God, pour out your Spirit upon us and upon these your gifts of bread and the fruit of the vine, that the bread we break and the cup we bless may be the communion of the body and blood of Christ. By your Spirit, make us one with all who work to fulfill your aims for the world. As you show us your grace in the breaking of bread and the sharing of the cup, help us become a community of conversation, open to a greater understanding of who you are and to what you ask of us, your creation.

We give you thanks that the Lord Jesus, on the night before he died, took bread, and after giving thanks to you, he broke it, and gave it to his disciples, saying: Take, eat. This is my body, given for you. Do this in remembrance of me.

In the same way he took the cup, saying: This cup is the new covenant, shed for you for the forgiveness of sins. Whenever you drink it, do this in remembrance of me.

Keep us faithful in your service until that day when all peoples shall remember and turn, and bow before you — that day when we join all people of faith to serve you with gladness and enter your presence with joy.

The gifts of God for the people of God.

Thanks be to God.

Prayer after Communion

God of all, we have been nourished by the gifts of creation. We now go, knowing that we can do our part to share and to listen, to proclaim our faith and to be silent when you choose to speak to us through the voice of the other, to question bravely and to live genuinely in a world that needs to see you at work in us. Amen.

Bibliography

_____. 2010 Census. http://www.census.gov/2010census (accessed November 30, 2017).

_____. "A Social Statement on Sufficient, Sustainable Livelihood for All by the ELCA." *ELCA*. 1999. https://www.elca.org/en/Faith/Faith-and-Society/Social-Statements/Economic-Life (accessed May 4, 2017).

_____. "What is Compassionate Resistance?" *Damsels in Defiance*. https://damselsindefiance.org/what-is-compassionate-resistance/ (accessed May 15, 2017).

_____. "Environmental Racism." *United Church of Christ*. http://www.ucc.org/environmentalministries_environmental-racism (accessed May 2, 2015).

_____. "Factoid: Black Male Incarceration Rate Is 6 Times Greater Than Rate for White Males." *All Other Persons*. November 3, 2009. http://allotherpersons.wordpress.com/2009/11/03/factoid-black-male-incarceration-rate-is-6-times-greater-than-rate-for-white-males (accessed May 3, 2017).

_____. "Haiku Poems About Prayer." http://www.haikupoemsandpoets.com/poems/prayer_haiku_poems (accessed May 6, 2017).

_____. "Is the Treatment the Cure? A Study of the Effects of Participation in Pastoral Leader Peer Groups." *Austin Presbyterian*

Seminary. April, 2010. https://www.samford.edu/uploaded-Files/RCPE/Content/ Is%20the%20Treatment%20the%20Cure.pdf (accessed November 30, 2017).

_____. "Marks of the Church." *Next Reformation*. http://nextreformation.com/?p=1435 (accessed November 30, 2017).

_____. "Pirke Avot 2:8." Ancient Wisdom for Us Today. http://ancientwisdom4ustoday.org/?page_id=844 (accessed May 5, 2017).

_____. "Poverty Guidelines." Health and Human Services. https://aspe.hhs.gov/poverty-guidelines (accessed May 4, 2017).

_____. Racial Predatory Loans Fueled U.S. Housing Crisis: Study." Reuters. October 4, 2010. http://www.reuters.com/article/2010/10/04/us-usa-foreclosures-race-idUSTRE6930K520101004 (accessed May 3, 2017).

_____. "Small Acts of Compassion," *Beliefnet* (June, 2005), http://www.beliefnet.com/wellness/health/2005/06/small-acts-of-compassion.aspx#cHJfEchmoJekoYPx.99 (accessed May 7, 2017).

_____. "SPLC Study Finds That More Than Half of States Fail at Teaching the Civil Rights Movement." *Southern Poverty Law Center*. https://www.splcenter.org/news/2011/09/28/splc-study-finds-more-half-states-fail-teaching-civil-rights-movement (accessed November 30, 2017).

_____. Sustaining Self-Care: a tool for personal awareness." *Training for Change*. https://www.trainingforchange.org/tools/sustaining- self-care-tool-personal-awareness (accessed May 5. 2017).

_____. "Syrian Children Under Siege." UNICEF. https://www.unicefusa.org/mission/emergencies/childrefugees/syria-crisis (accessed May 5, 2017).

_____. "United Nations Peacekeeping Operations Principles and Guidelines." New York: United Nations Department of Peacekeeping Operations and Department of Field Support, 2008.

_____. "The Confession of 1967." *The Constitution of the Presbyterian Church (USA) Part I: The Book of Confessions.* Louisville: Office of the General Assembly, 2003. 9.18.

_____. "Violence." The American Psychological Association http://www.apa.org/topics/violence/ (accessed January 12, 2018).

_____. "Voices from Syria." *Peace and Conflict Monitor.* October 10, 2014. http://www.monitor.upeace.org/innerpg.cfm?id_article=1067 (accessed May 5, 2017).

Barnes-Josiah, Debora. "Undoing Racism in Public Health: A Blueprint for Action in Urban MCH." University of Nebraska Medical Center. August 1, 2004. http://webmedia.unmc.edu/Community/ CityMatch/CityMatCHUndoingRacismReport.pdf (accessed May 3, 2017).

Barth, Karl. Church *Dogmatics, Vol. III:* 4. Edinburgh: T&T Clark, 1958.

Bayer, Charles H. *A Guide to Liberation Theology for Middle Class Congregations.* Eugene, OR: Wipf & Stock, 1986.

Beck, Richard. "The Paradoxes of Progressive Political Theology: The Paradox Revisited." *Experimental Theology.* May 11, 2017. http://experimentaltheology.blogspot.co.uk/2017/05/the-paradoxes-of-progressive-political_11.html (accessed January 12, 2018).

Blackman, Andrew. "Can Money Buy You Happiness?" *WSJ.* November 10, 2014. https://www.wsj.com/articles/ can-money-buy-happiness-heres-what-science-has-to-say-1415569538 (accessed May 4, 2017).

Braha, Bender. "Experiential Torah." *Arachim.* http://arachimusa.org/ArticleDetail.asp?ArticleID=1635 (accessed May 5, 2017).

Blankley, Bethany. "The Oxymoron of Christian Protest." *The Christian Post.* April 23, 2012. http://www.christianpost.com/news/the-oxymoron-of-christian-protest-73704/ (accessed May 4, 2017).

Bloch, Ernst, Jamie Owen Daniel, Tom Moylan, eds. *Not Yet.* London: Verso, 1997.

Bly, Robert. *The Kabir Book: Forty-four of the Ecstatic Poems of Kabir.* Boston: Beacon Press, 1977.

Branson, Mark Lau. "Forming God's People." http://www.alban.org/conversation (accessed May 15, 2015).

Bright, John. *The Kingdom of God.* New York: Abingdon, 1953.

Buber, Martin "Gandhi, the Jews & Zionism: Martin Buber's Open Letter to Gandhi Regarding Palestine." *Jewish Virtual Library.* February 24, 1939. http://www.jewishvirtuallibrary.org/letter-from-martin-buber-to-gandhi (accessed January 12, 2018).

Burke, Alan. "Police: Mother Asks Officers to Arrest Her Squabbling Children." *The Salem News.* January 12, 2012. http://www.salemnews.com/local/x191087269/Police-Mother-asks-officers-to-arrest-her-squabbling-children (accessed May 4, 2017).

Camus, Albert. *The Rebel: An Essay on Man in Revolt,* Anthony Bower, trans. New York: Vintage International, 1956.

Carlson, Lauren K. "Room for Hope: Why Justice Work Needs Contemplation," *Sojourners.* Oct. 12, 2016. https://sojo.net/articles/room-hope-why-social-justice-needs-contemplation (accessed May 6, 2017).

Cloke, Kenneth; Joan Goldsmith. *Resolving Conflicts at Work: Eight Strategies for Everyone on the Job.* San Francisco: Jossey-Bass, 2005.

Cooke, Kristina; David Rhode; Ryan McNeil. "The Undeserving Poor." *The Atlantic.* Dec. 20, 2012. https://www.theatlantic.com/business/archive/2012/12/the-undeserving-poor/266507/ (accessed November 30, 2017).

Coover, Virginia, et al. *Resource Manual for a Living Revolution.* British Columbia: New Society Press: 1978.

Damico, Linda H. *The Anarchist Dimension of Liberation Theology.* Eugene, OR: Wipf & Stock, 1989.

Dellinger, Drew. "Hieroglyphic Staircase." September 29, 2009. http://drewdellinger.org/pages/ video/187/hieroglyphic-stairway (accessed May 4, 2017).

Dickinson, Emily. " 'Hope is the things with feathers." The Poetry Foundation. https://www.poetryfoundation.org / poems-and-poets/poems/detail/42889 (accessed May 7, 2017).

Dionne, E.J, Jr.; William A. Galston; Korin Davis; Ross Tilchin. "Faith in Equality: Economic Justice and the Future of Religious Progressives." *Brookings*. Washington, DC: Brookings, 2014.

Eichrodt, Walter. *Theology of the Old Testament, vol. 1*. Philadelphia: Westminster, 1961.

Ewall, Mike. "Legal Tools for Environmental Equity vs. Environmental Justice." October 15, 2012. http://www.ejnet.org/ej/ejlaw.pdf (accessed May 3, 2017).

Everist, Norma Cook. Church Conflict: From Contention to Collaboration. Nashville: Abingdon, 2004.

Fisher, Len. The Perfect Swarm: The Science of Complexity in Everyday Life. New York: Basic Books, 2009.

Fischer, Noah. "Occupying Tension." 2012. http://inquiringmind.com/Articles/OccupyingTension.html (accessed May 1, 2015).

Forest, Jim. *Loving Our Enemies: Reflections on the Hardest Commandment*. Maryknoll, NY: Orbis Press, 2014.

Frankle, Victor. *Man's Search for Meaning*. New York: Pocket, 1959.

Gayatso, Tenzin, the Fourteenth Dalai Lama. The *Compassionate Life*. Boston: Wisdom, 2003.

Grimsrud, Ted. "Healing Justice: A Sermon." *Peace Theology*. January 18, 2009. http://peacetheology.net/pacifism/healing-justice-a-sermon/ (accessed May 4, 2017).

Guenther Loewen, Susanne. "Is God a Pacifist? The A. James Reimer and J. Denny Weaver Debate in

Contemporary Mennonite Peace Theology." *The Conrad Grebel Review*, 33:3. Fall, 2015.

Havel, Vaclav. "Speak Truth to Power." *RFK Center for Justice and Human Rights*. 2010. http://blogs.nysut.org/sttp/defenders/vaclav-havel (accessed May 4, 2017).

Hirschfield, Brad. *You Don't Have to be Wrong for Me to be Right: Finding Faith Without Fanaticism*. New York: Harmony, 2009.

Hirshfield, Jane. "For What Binds Us." *Poetry Foundation*. http://www.poetryfoundation.org/poem/186177. (accessed May 5, 2017).

Hoban, Jack E., Bruce J. Gourlie. "The Ethical Warrior: Protecting Our Enemies." *PoliceOne*. December 19, 2011. http://www.policeone.com/close-quarters-combat/articles/4836574-The-ethical-warrior-Protecting-our-enemies/ (accessed May 4, 2017).

Holladay, William L. *Long Ago God Spoke: How Christians May Hear the Old Testament Today*. Minneapolis: Augsburg, 1995.

Humphreys, Keith. "There's been a big decline in the black incarceration rate, and almost nobody's paying attention." *Washington Post*. Feb. 10, 2016. https://www.washingtonpost.com/news/wonk/wp/2016/02/10/almost-nobody-is-paying-attention-to-this-massive-change-in-criminal-justice/?utm_term=.cccd24274e5f (accessed November 30, 2017).

Jantzen, Grace M. "Roots of Violence, Seeds of Peace." *The Conrad Grebel Review*, 20:2. Spring, 2002.

Jenkins, Jack. "The Rise of The Religious Left: Religious Progressives Will Soon Outnumber Conservatives." *Think Progress*. July 19, 2013. http://thinkprogress.org/politics/2013/07/19/2324411/the-rise-of-the-religious-left-religious-progressives-will-soon-outnumber-conservatives/ (accessed May 2, 2017).

Jones, Jeffery. "On Social Ideology, the Left Catches Up to the Right." May 21, 2015. http://www.gallup.com/poll/183386/

social-ideology-left-catches-right.aspx?utm_source=Politics& utm_medium=newsfeed&utm_campaign=tiles (accessed May 2, 2017).

Jones, Robert. "Self-Segregation: Why It's So Hard for Whites to Understand Ferguson." *The Atlantic*. August 21, 2014. http://www.theatlantic.com/national/archive/2014/08/self-segregation-why-its-hard-for-whites-to-understand-ferguson/378928/ (accessed May 3, 2017).

Kauffman, Ivan J. "Nonviolence Works — If Somebody Does the Work." *The Conrad Grebel Review*, 20:2. Spring, 2002.

King, Martin Luther, Jr. "Remaining Awake Through a Great Revolution." *King Encyclopedia*. April 9, 1968. http://mlkkpp01.stanford.edu/index.php/encyclopedia/documentsentry/doc_remaining_awake_through_a_great_revolution/ (accessed May 1, 2015).

Kivel, Paul. *Uprooting Racism: How White People Can Work for Racial Justice*. Philadelphia, PA: New Society Publishers, 1995.

Law, Eric. *Inclusion: Making Room for Grace*. St. Louis: Chalice, 2000.

Madland, David. "Making Our Middle Class Stronger." *Center for American Progress*. August 1, 2012. http://www.americanprogress.org/issues/economy/report/2012/08/01/12034/making-our-middle-class-stronger/ (accessed November 30, 3017).

Marin, Andrew. "Belong, Believe, Become." *Love Is an Orientation*. http://www.patheos.com/blogs/loveisanorientation/2011/02/belong-believe-become/#ixzz3RA6w9IDt (accessed May 7, 2017).

Marks, Julia. *The Value of Sparrows: Writings of a Christian Mystic*. https://thevalueofsparrows.com/2012/11/12/prayer-a-prayer-for-friends-and-a-prayer-for-enemies-by-anselm/ (accessed May 3, 2017).

Marler, Penny Long, et al. *So Much Better: How Thousands of Pastors Help Each Other Thrive*. St. Louis: Chalice Press, 2013.

Marsh, Michael K. "Theosis, the Human Vocation." *Interrupting the Silence*. July 9, 2011. https://interruptingthesilence.com/2011/07/09/theosis-the-human-vocation/ (accessed May 5, 2017).

McCarthy, Emmanuel Charles. "The Nonviolent Eucharistic Jesus: A Pastoral Approach." *Center for Christian Nonviolence*. http://www.centerforchristiannonviolence.org/data/Media/NV_Eucharist_ PastoralApproach_01d.pdf, (accessed March 19, 2016).

McKenzie, Alyce M. "The Faith of a Soldier: Reflections on Luke 7:1-10," *Patheos*. May 26, 2013. http://www.patheos.com/Progressive-Christian/Faith-Soldier-Alyce-McKenzie-05-27-2013 (accessed Aug. 30, 2016).

Merton, Thomas. *New Seeds of Contemplation*. New York: New Directions, 1961.

Miller, Peter. "Swarm Theory." National Geographic Magazine. July 1, 2007. http://ngm.nationalgeographic.com/2007/07/swarms/miller-text (accessed November 30, 2017).

Miller, Peter. *The Smart Swarm: How Understanding Flocks, Schools, and Colonies Can Make Us Better at Communicating, Decision Making, and Getting Things Done*. New York: Avery, 2010.

Murray, Stuart. *Post Christendom: Church and Mission in a Strange New World*. Milton Keynes: Paternoster, 2004.

Newell, John Philip. *A New Harmony: The Spirit, the Earth, and the Human Soul*. San Francisco: Jossey-Bass, 2011.

Newport, Frank. "Americans Have Widespread Personal Financial Concerns." *Gallup*. http://www.gallup.com/poll/117817/americans-widespread-personal-financial-concerns.aspx (accessed May 4, 2017).

Nichols, Stephen J. *Jesus Made in America: A Cultural History from the Puritans to The Passion of the Christ.* Downer's Grove: IVP, 2008.

Niewold, Jack. "Set Theory in Leadership." *Journal of Biblical Perspectives in Leadership* 2, no. 1. Winter 2008.

Nietzsche, Friedrich. *Human All Too Human: a Book for Free Spirits.* Lexido.com. http://www.lexido.com/EBOOK_TEXTS/HUMAN_ALL_TOO_HUMAN_BOOK_ONE_.aspx?S=71 (accessed May 7, 2017).

Pender, William C. "Giving Up Something Bad for Lent." 3/9/2014. *First Presbyterian Church of Knoxville.* http://www.fpcknox.org/site/wp-content/uploads/2014/03/Sermon-3-9-2014-Pender.pdf (accessed May 7, 2017).

Philip, T.V. "Christian Spirituality (1 Corinthians 1:18-25)." *Religion Online.* http://www.religiononline.org/showarticle.asp?title=1539 (accessed May 2, 2017).

Plummer, Deborah. *Racing Across the Lines: Changing Race Relations Through Friendship.* Cleveland: Pilgrim Press, 2004.

Pope Francis. "Transcript: Pope Francis's speech to Congress." *The Washington Post* (Sept. 24, 2015). https://www.washingtonpost.com/local/social-issues/transcript-pope-franciss-speech-to-congress/2015/09/24/6d7d7ac8-62bf-11e5-8e9e-dce8a2a2a679_story.html?utm_term=.695b917ce211 (accessed May 18, 2017).

Pratt, David "War or Peace? Thinking Outside the Box." *Tricycle Magazine.* Spring, 2002. https://tricycle.org/magazine/war-or-peace-thinking-outside-the-box/ (accessed January 12, 2018).

Putnam, Robert D. "E Pluribus Unum: Diversity and Community in the Twenty-first Century." *Scandinavian Political Studies*, Vol. 30, No. 2, 2007.

Reich, Robert B. "The Political Roots of Widening Inequality." *The American Prospect*, 26:2. Spring, 2015.

Rendle, Gil. *Behavioral Covenants in Congregations.* Herndon, VA: Alban Institute, 1999.

Robertson, David. "Comment: New Secularism Is an Attempt to Undermine and Destroy Christianity." *Christianity Today.* May 19, 2014. http://www.christiantoday.com/article/comment. new.secularism.is.an.attempt. to.undermine.and.destroy.christianity/ 37537.htm (accessed May 2, 2017).

Rice, S. "Non-violent conflict management: Conflict resolution, dealing with anger, and negotiation and mediation." Berkeley: University of California at Berkeley, California Social Work Education Center, 2002.

Roach, David "Poll: Many Pastors Feel Lonely, Discouraged." *Pastors.com.* October 24, 2011. http://pastors.com/poll-many-pastors-feel-lonely-discouraged/ (accessed May 5, 2017).

Robert A Rimbo. *Why Worship Matters.* Minneapolis: Augsburg, 2004.

Shapiro, Ilana. "A Guide to Selected Programs for Racial Equity Inclusion." *Aspen Institute.* 2002. http://www.aspeninstitute. org /sites/default/files/content/docs/rcc/training.pdf (accessed November 30, 2017).

Sheldrake, Rupert. *The Presence of the Past: Morphic Resonance and the Habits of Nature.* London: Icon, 2011.

Sherwin, Byron L. *Faith Finding Meaning: A Theology of Judaism.* Oxford: Oxford University Press, 2009.

Tippett, Krista. *Einstein's God: Conversations about Science and the Human Spirit.* New York: Penguin Books, 2010.

Tiller, Robert. "Faithing." *Christ Congregational Church.* August 23, 2015. http://www.cccsilverspring.org/sermons/sermon-for-august-23-2015?rq=tiller (accessed 9 May, 2016).

Volf, Miroslav. *Exclusion and Embrace.* Nashville: Abingdon, 1996.

Warren, Dorian T. "Putting Families First: Good Jobs for All." *Center for Community Change, et. al.* 2015.

Weaver, J. Denny. *The Nonviolent God*. Grand Rapids: Eerdmans, 2013.

Wheatley, Margaret J., Geoff Crinean. "Solving, not Attacking, Complex Problems: A Five-State Approach Based on an Ancient Practice." 2004. http://www.margaretwheatley.com/articles/solvingnotattacking.html (accessed January 12, 2018).

Wilson, Jayne. "Treating Proud Flesh: Excessive Granulation Tissue in Horses." *MyHorse.com*. http://myhorse.com/blogs/horse-care/illness-and-injuries/proud-flesh-in-horses/ (accessed May 19, 2015).

Yancey, Eddie. "Rhythm and Blues protest songs: voices of resistance." *ETD Collection for AUC Robert W. Woodruff Library, Paper 610*. Atlanta: Clark Atlanta University, 2007.

Also from Energion Publications
Guides to Practical Ministry

In this clear, concise and hope-filled book Ruth Fletcher offers substantive help and direction to congregational leaders and pastors alike. Grounded in her years of experience in a wide variety of church settings, her faithful observation of human life and her deep love of God, Ruth tells us stories of transformation that arise like green shoots from the most unexpected and unlikely of places.

Rev. Laurie Rudel
Pastor, Queen Anne
Christian Church
Seattle, Washington

From another
Academy of Parish Clergy author

Bob Cornwall provides a vision for today's Christians, centered around living out our gifts in creative and life-transforming ways. We are gifted, even when we are unaware of it.

Bruce Epperly, PhD
Pastor and Author

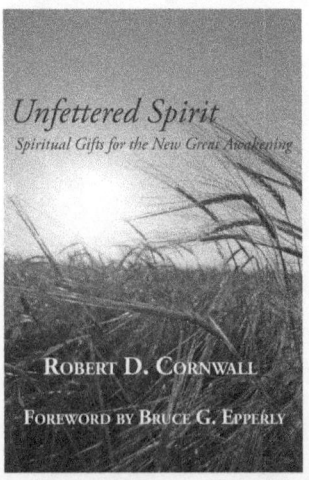

More from Energion Publications

Academy of Parish Clergy Series and Authors

Conversations in Ministry
Clergy Table Talk	Kent Ira Groff	$9.99
Out of the Office	Robert D. Cornwall	$9.99
Wind and Whirlwind	David Moffett-Moore	$9.99

Guides to Practical Ministry
Overcoming Sermon Block	William Powell Tuck	$12.99
Thrive	Ruth Fletcher	$14.99
In Changing Times	Ron Higdon	$14.99

Academy Member Authors (Selected Titles)
Faith in the Public Square	Robert D. Cornwall	$16.99
Ephesians: A Participatory Study Guide		$9.99
Ultimate Allegiance		$9.99
The Authority of Scripture in a Postmodern Age		$5.99
From Words of Woe to Unbelievable News		$5.99
The Eucharist		$5.99
Unfettered Spirit		$14.99
From Here to Eternity	Bruce Epperly	$5.99
Angels, Mysteries, and Miracles		$9.99
Transforming Acts		$14.99
Jonah: When God Changes		$5.99
Process Theology: Embracing Adventure with God		$5.99
The Journey to the Undiscovered Country	William Powell Tuck	$9.99
Lord, I Keep Getting a Busy Signal		$9.99
The Last Words from the Cross		$9.99
The Church Under the Cross		$9.99
Creation in Contemporary Experience	David Moffett-Moore	$9.99
Life as Pilgrimage		$14.99
The Spirit's Fruit		$9.99
The Jesus Manifesto		$9.99
Spiritual Care Reflections	Charles J. Lopez, Jr.	$14.99
Surviving a Son's Suicide	Ron Higdon	$9.99
All I Need to Know I'm Still Learning at 80		

Generous Quantity Discounts Available
Dealer Inquiries Welcome
Energion Publications — P.O. Box 841
Gonzalez, FL_ 32560
Website: http://energionpubs.com
Phone: (850) 525-3916

www.ingramcontent.com/pod-product-compliance
Lightning Source LLC
LaVergne TN
LVHW090115080426
835507LV00040B/890